The Birch Creek Hangings
and other Montana Tales
from Choteau to Glacier Park

The remarkable people, weather, crimes and events that made the local weekly news.

Also by Nancy C. Thornton

**Tales from
Montana's Rocky Mountain Front**

Tales from Montana's Teton County

Tales from Choteau Montana

The Birch Creek Hangings
and other Montana Tales
from Choteau to Glacier Park

*The remarkable people, weather, crimes and
events that made the local weekly news.*

Nancy C. Thornton

**Canal Heritage Enterprises
Choteau, Montana
2020**

Cover Design: Ralph Thornton.
Front Cover Top: Iconic Red Buses along Going to the Sun Road, Copyright
Ralph Thornton, 2014. Bottom: HPF 9518: Old mining town of Altyn,
near Many Glacier. View of bridge and buildings in town. Copied from the
Dean Collection in the Glacier National Park Archives. Used by permission.
Unknown photographer, taken ca. 1904. Inset Photograph: Broken comb and
crockery items lying at the former site of Altyn. Copyright Nancy C. Thornton,
2015.

Back Cover: The headwaters of Cattle Queen Creek in Glacier National Park,
Copyright Ralph Thornton, 2019. Inset photograph of the author, Copyright
Nancy C. Thornton, 2019.

The stories for this volume were written by Nancy C. Thornton and were
originally published in the Choteau Acantha weekly newspaper. This volume
has minor edits in the text for clarity. Grateful acknowledgment is made to
the Choteau Acantha for permission to use copyrighted material.

First Printing: 2020

ISBN 978-0-9700704-6-3

Canal Heritage Enterprises
P.O. Box 1482
Choteau MT 59422
www.canalheritage.com

Contents

Acknowledgements

I would like to thank the Choteau Acantha publishers, Jeff and Melody Martinsen, and my husband, Ralph Thornton, without whose help this book would never have been completed. 🏔

Preface

"...news is history in its first and best form, its vivid and fascinating form, and...history is the pale and tranquil reflection of it." — *Mark Twain's Autobiography*

My interest in local history was honed by spending more than 25 years living near the small community of Lemont, Illinois, in the Illinois and Michigan Canal National Heritage Corridor, a narrowly-defined geographic area with a rich history and a few century-old local newspapers that documented that history.

After moving to Choteau, Montana, with my husband, Ralph, in 1999, I became intrigued by that same intensely local focus that the Choteau Acantha newspaper brought to its readers. I became a subscriber to and an employee of the Acantha.

The Choteau Acantha's "local news" focus is and always has been a paramount goal of its succession of publishers and editors since 1894. And so, the merging of my interest in the local history of the Rocky Mountain Front, Teton County and its county seat of Choteau naturally developed after reading the old newspapers of the region. They memorialize the history of the communities along the Front as does no other resource.

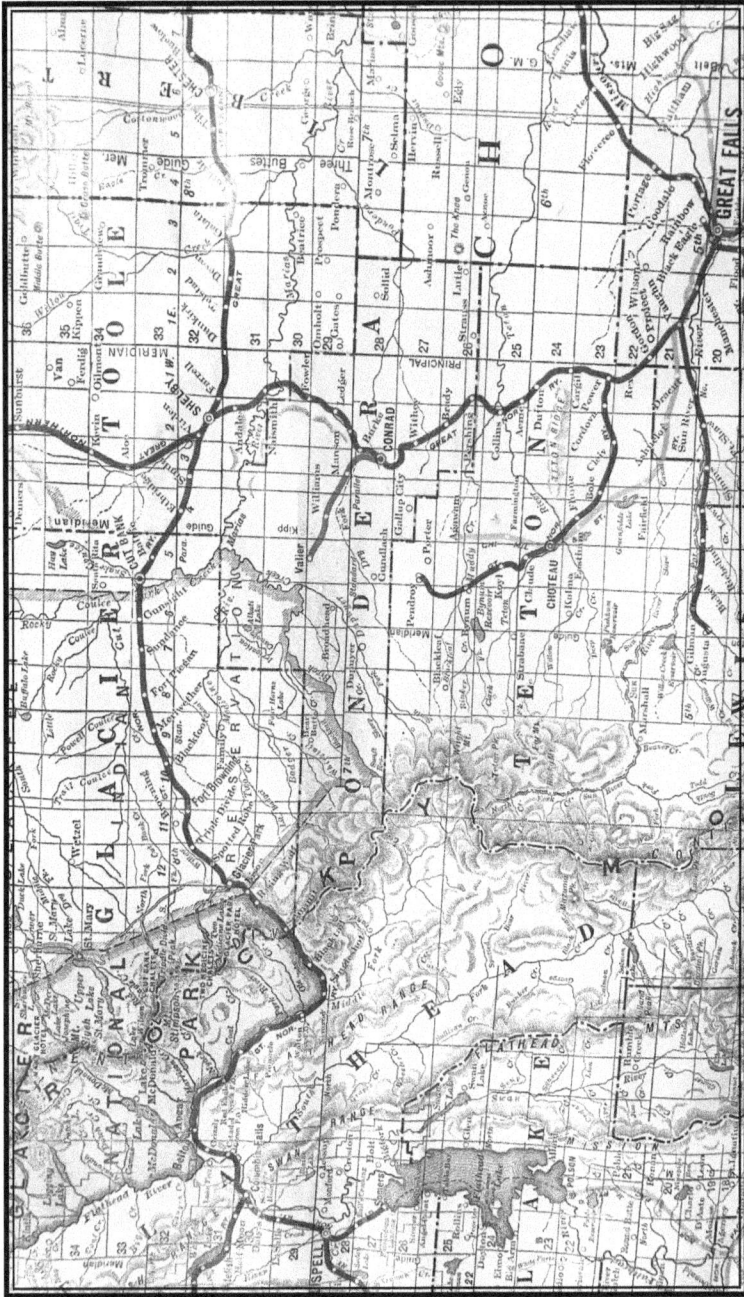

Map of the Great Northern Railway circa 1923. Source: Havre Railway Museum collection, 2018.

Introduction

The mostly treeless prairies and foothills along the Rocky Mountain Front from the small city of Choteau north to Glacier National Park offer scenic expanses on good weather days, and dangerous ground blizzards on bad ones.

The tales that follow are mostly about the people, events and places in the northern region of northcentral Montana, including Choteau, Glacier National Park and the Helena-Lewis and Clark National Forest west of Choteau. The stories are true, or as true as the newspaper editors of the past believed to be true. Here and there the editors of the day left out information deemed too sensitive for their readers and those details are now lost to history.

The oldest stories in this volume are gleaned from research in Helena and Fort Benton newspapers. Starting about 1885, Choteau had its own newspaper, as did Dupuyer for 10 years starting in 1894. The news reports expanded each year as pioneer settlements developed: Sun River, Old Agency, Choteau, Bynum, Dupuyer, Valier, Altyn and a handful of other communities. Early reports came in from the Blackfeet Reservation and later reports detailed the beginnings of Glacier National Park.

Promoters who wanted to split up Montana's original Chouteau County proposed the name "Teton" County in the 1880s. Resistance to the breakup delayed approval of the split in the state Legislature until March 1, 1893. The new county extended from the Sun River to the Canadian border. The western boundary was the Continental Divide. The eastern boundary included townships halfway to Fort Benton, Chouteau County's county seat, and it took a few more fights in 1914, 1919, and 1921 before the current boundaries were settled.

For convention sake, this volume uses "Choteau" for the city in Teton County platted in 1883, and "Chouteau" to refer to the county from which Teton County was created in 1893. However, readers should note that they were once spelled the same. The state Legislature did not add the inside "u" to differentiate the county's name until March 5, 1903. (The story of Choteau's name is published in "Tales from the Rocky Mountain Front.")

That book captures stories from the 1870s to 1935, including the birth of Choteau. The book, "Tales from Montana's Teton County," captures stories from the 1920s to the 2000s, and "Tales from Choteau Montana," captures stories generated about and near the city of Choteau.

Readers have enjoyed these old news tales published in the weekly Choteau Acantha newspaper since 1999. This fourth volume introduces new readers to the local history of the region north of Choteau for the most part.

For readers who want to read the original newspaper pages, visit the Montana Historical Society's website, www.montananewspapers.org. To read the current Choteau Acantha, visit the website, www.choteauacantha.com.

This book presents a collection of previously published stories highlighting local history, in mostly chronological order based on the year generally taken from story's subject matter. The date under the chapter title is the date the Acantha published them. Some text in this volume was edited or condensed from the original "It's old news" columns for clarity and to correct errors and conserve space as needed.

The Birch Creek Hangings

The first report of the lynchings on Birch Creek was in the April 2, 1885, Sun River Sun newspaper, but let's start with an introduction to someone who was associated, rightly or wrongly, with the incident as recently as a mention in the 1977 Dupuyer Centennial book, "By Gone Days and Modern Ways."

Enlisted man Frank H. Federhen was a musician, an inventor, a bookkeeper, a newspaper correspondent and a justice of the peace during his life, so an allegation that he took part in a lynching deserves some exploration.

Federhen was honorably discharged from the Army on Dec. 14, 1884, at Helena. He had been a battalion sergeant major under General John K. Brooke in the 3rd U.S. Infantry at the time of the 1876 election riots in New Orleans and he served at Fort Logan in Meagher County before he was mustered out at age 32.

A native of Massachusetts, Federhen got a job as a bookkeeper at the J.W. McKnight Trading Post in Dupuyer. He also started writing a weekly column for Fort Benton's River Press newspaper in February 1885. He signed his columns with the name, "Kanapsa" from Birch Creek.

During the month before the hanging, Kanapsa wrote about a burglary at Charles Thomas's saloon, a wedding and that the local priest had gathered 13 Indian youngsters to live and be taught at St. Peter's Mission on the Blackfeet Reservation.

The Sun River Sun's sardonic telling of the lynching was tinged with callousness that is verboten in local newspapers today.

The headline ran, "Two horse thieves hung. Birch Creek the scene of a neck-tie party last Thursday — opening the season rather early."

The story: "The annual free-pass-over-the-range season for horse thieves has opened rather early this year and should prove a warning to all others to desist before being compelled to do so by means of a rope in the hands of a few resolute men. Birch Creek lays claim to the honor of hoisting the first of the season, which occurred last Thursday, the particulars of which were furnished us by a friend.

"On Wednesday of last week two men, bearing the names of Felix and MacDonald, (later McDonald) made their appearance in Dupuyer, claiming to hail from Fort Macleod, Northwest Territory, and were looking for purchasers for a number of head of horses and mules, which they had with them. The bringing of horses from the Northwest Territory into Montana is something very unusual, and created a suspicion at once in the minds of the good people of Dupuyer that all was not right, and a party of four, well mounted, started after the horse traders, for the purpose of making an investigation, and overtook them at Birch Creek, and in answer to their inquires concerning the stock were given no satisfaction.

"The Dupuyer parties considered their actions suspicious enough to warrant their arrest, but the traders thought otherwise, and as a precautionary measure, took possession of Kipp & Thomas's saloon, which was nearby, and defied arrest. The pursuing party, although in the majority, thought it best to be discreet, and after posting sentinels to prevent the escape of the birds, secured the reinforcement of some 20 men armed with Winchesters, and the next morning turned them loose on the shack. After the first volley the besieged displayed a flag of truce, and marched out into the hands of the 'committee.'

"After a thorough and impartial investigation it was shown beyond a doubt that the men were horse thieves, and that the stock in their possession was stolen. It was decided to take them to Benton, and there give them the benefit of the law, but one of the party, known as Felix, declined the hospitality furnished at the jail, and give his captors to understand that he would rather 'camp on the trail,' and the magnanimity of the Birch and Dupuyer people — which knows no bounds — kindly consented to the change, and also consented to allow his partner to 'camp' with him.

"They accepted an invitation extended to them by the committee to take an active part in a neck-tie sociable during the day, and consequently they were given a decent burial about one mile above the store on Birch Creek last Saturday at 10 a.m."

That was the first version. The news was quickly picked up in other papers including the Dillon Tribune and the Billings Herald. The River Press in Fort Benton reported on the Birch Creek lynching on April 8, 1885. It was the second version of the incident, following the report in the April 2 Sun River Sun.

It read: "Hung High. A couple of horse thieves and desperadoes strung up at Birch Creek for their wickedness. From M.S. Rickard, who returned last evening from Birch Creek, our reporter obtained the following particulars regarding the hanging of two horse thieves and desperadoes at Birch Creek on the morning of Thursday last:

"Two men, Felix Constant and McDonald, came from the north a few days ago, bringing with them eight large mules belonging to the Northwestern Coal Co. and a lot of horses belonging to various parties, in all 20 or more head of stock. They made strong efforts to dispose of them and had induced a ranchman on Dupuyer Creek to buy the mules for $1,000.

"The sale was not consummated, however, owing to the fact that no one would make out a bill of sale for them, and they had no bill of sale from the northern owners of the animals. This fact aroused the suspicion that the stock had been stolen, and it was determined to arrest the men and bring them to Benton.

"The fact of the contemplated arrest reached their ears and they determined not to be taken, and barricaded themselves in a room back of the saloon. Felix said he would never surrender alive, and McDonald would surrender if they would produce a warrant. The number of men in the immediate vicinity did not feel justified in forcing a surrender. This was on Wednesday, and the men were allowed to remain in the building, which was guarded to prevent their escape. Messengers were sent to Dupuyer and up and down Birch Creek, and by noon there were fully 50 persons present.

"The men were again summoned to surrender but refused, Felix still saying he would not be taken alive. After a while, McDonald came to the side door and with his hand on his pistol said they would surrender; but as he was prepared to do someone harm, his answer was a volley from the Winchesters of the guards — about 20 shots were fired, none taking effect.

"In a couple of hours he again came to the door with a flag of truce and his hands up, closely followed by Felix. They were speedily disarmed and chained to the logs of the room, the chinking being knocked out to admit the chain going around the logs. They were told that they would be taken to Benton, but they wanted to be taken to Helena.

"Felix again said he would not be taken alive to Benton.

They told their captors they would yet get even with the entire party and boldly announced their intention to kill every one of them.

"They were under guard the rest of the day, and late at night Chas. Thomas and Rickard were on guard. About 2 o'clock Thursday morning Rickard, hearing a noise, turned suddenly around and found himself facing a mob of between 30 and 40 masked men. He made a show of resistance but was knocked down, his arms and legs pinioned, gagged and dragged through the snow about 150 feet from the building and left there.

"Thomas was not treated quite so roughly, but he was bound and gagged. The crowd then went into the room, took the prisoners out, carried them about a half mile up the creek and hung them to a convenient tree. Rickard did not hear that they made any confession. He lay on the snow in the storm about four hours before he was liberated. He was bound so tightly that it was several hours before circulation was restored. His thumb was broken, and that, together with the blow from the gun, which knocked him down, left him somewhat used up. ... Of the mob he says he never saw a more resolute set of men. They went to work systematically, and during the whole time not a word was uttered. ... In the absence of a coroner a jury of citizens was empaneled, who viewed the bodies and brought in a verdict, the substance of which we have not learned."

The River Press's Birch Creek correspondent, Kanapsa, the pen name for Frank H. Federhen of Dupuyer, published his own version and a defense of the March 26 lynching.

Horse theft was rampant on Montana's open range. About a year before this incident, vigilantes had hanged 13 men, five at one time at Rocky Point on the Missouri below Fort Benton. Another seven men were reportedly hanged a month later at the mouth of the Musselshell River.

The River Press on April 8 printed a news story along with Kanapsa's version. His telling, dated two days after the hangings, starts with details, but ends with a defense for the action taken.

His column read, "Again I am called upon to chronicle to you an event of excitement here on Birch Creek, but this time, I am sorry to say, not one of pleasure, but one of sadness, and one which fills our hearts, no matter how salutary its effects, with horror, and this is the lynching of two men named Edward McDonald and Felix Constanes on the night of the 25th inst.

"These men came here with eight head of mules and eight or 10 horses to sell. They went to Dupuyer Creek on the 24th and endeavored to sell the animals, or part of them, to Dr. Henry Gillette, and not succeeding, made another effort to sell them to James Pierce, who asked them for a bill of sale, refusing to buy until it could be produced. The animals had been left on Birch Creek, and the men promised to have them at Dupuyer with a bill of sale by 10 o'clock the next day.

"While at Dupuyer, the men had told three different stories as to the manner in which they had obtained possession of the stock, and the suspicions of the people of Dupuyer having become aroused, five of them came over in the evening (McDonald and his partner preceding them by an hour or two) and entering the store were just in time to catch McDonald making out a bill of sale to cover his possession of the mules.

"Upon the arrival of the Dupuyer party, the men instantly left the store and hurried over to Thomas's saloon, where they had left their revolvers (Thomas was at the store), and took possession. Joe Kipp, deputy sheriff, asked them to surrender, but they refused, saying they defied anyone to come and take them.

"A guard was kept on the place that night, the men making two or three efforts to escape, but were fired at. The next morning messengers were sent to Dupuyer and the surrounding country, and by 10 o'clock about 35 men were on the spot.

"Before this reinforcement arrived, the thieves had threatened to come out and clean up the outfit, etc., but when they saw the number of men congregating, they surrendered. They were then put in the saloon and chained, and a guard placed over them. During the day Felix made a number of threats as to the revenge he would have should he get out of jail.

"Some time between one and two o'clock on the morning of the 26th the guard was overpowered and pretty roughly handled by masked men and the prisoners taken out and hung. The next morning a passer-by, seeing the bodies, reported the fact at the store. A coroner's jury was formed and the bodies cut down during the day and buried.

"These men were both of desperate character. The man, Felix, murdered a man on the Musselshell in May 1879 for money, and was known there as a horse thief and desperado. McDonald killed a man on the Musselshell about 1880, but this was done in self-defense. He, however, killed another man there about 1872 whose horses he had stolen. The man was trying to reclaim his animals when McDonald shot him.

"McDonald is known to the writer of this as a stage robber and horse thief. Both the men acknowledged to some of the guardsmen, during the day, that the stock was 'crooked' and was stolen from the Coal Navigation Co. of the Northwest Territory."

How did Kanapsa/Federhen know so much about the suspects only two days after the lynching? His association with the mob action and his defense of it became a story passed down by several Dupuyer and Birch Creek families.

Kanapsa's defense of the lynching ran over 1,000 words.

He said, "Utterly abhorrent as is the principle of lynching, I cannot say one word against the men who were engaged in this affair. These men were known to be murderers and horse thieves. This is not mere hearsay, but is an actual fact, which is known to men here who have met and heard of them in other parts of the territory.

"Had James Pierce bought the mules he would have been out about $1,000, and the probabilities are the rascals would have helped themselves to stock here and driven it north. Many, both here and in the east, may say that this was done by a drunken mob, but it is not so.

"So far as my observations went during the day and night, not a single man (and there were about 25 here) showed the slightest tendency to become excited or drunk.

"In fact, everyone was cool and calm, and I believe that the deed was done deliberately and from a sense of duty to themselves and a necessity of protection to life and property. It is true enough there is a law in this country for the judgment and punishment of criminals, but how much protection have we, far out on the frontier, from this law? There is but one way, and that is, to protect ourselves. When an Indian can make his escape from the Benton jail, what confidence can we feel in consigning two desperadoes like these to its keeping — men who would be actuated by every motive and desire of revenge to make their escape and injure the men who were instrumental in effecting their capture?

"Do not think that I am endeavoring to shield the men who did this hanging, or that I am upholding the principles of lynching, for I am not. I am only trying to look the matter squarely in the face and get at the truth, distasteful and disagreeable as that truth may appear.

"I repeat, there is a law in this country, and every man

has a right to its benefits, but at the same time, where that law is so poorly enforced that all confidence in its protection to law-abiding citizens is lost, then I believe those citizens have a right to take the matter in their own hands and protect themselves.

"More than this: had these men been less firmly dealt with, it would have encouraged others of the same class to come across the line with stolen horses, and in a short time the people here would have been overrun with a gang of horse thieves and desperadoes, and God knows, we have enough to do to get along with the Indians without being subjected to the rascalities of these villains.

"Yes, it is well enough to sit in house or office, in town or city, and cry 'horror' when news is received of Judge Lynch's work, and to us on the frontier it always brings a feeling of sadness, but you are surrounded by the guardians of law and order, while our only protection consists in our individual reputation for strength and courage.

"And are we to submit to having our horses stolen, our lives placed in jeopardy by a lot of desperadoes? What chance does a law-abiding citizen stand with these villains?

"Suppose these men had been taken to Benton, they would not have stayed there long. Do you suppose they would have forgotten the men who took an active part in their arrest? No: they both have the red hands of murderers. They have been driven from the Musselshell, the Yellowstone, from Benton and Missoula; in fact, from the territory to Canada, by their crimes, and even in the latter place were watched and looked upon as bad characters. They came here with stock they acknowledged to have stolen, and tried to cheat an honest man out of his money by means of a forged bill of sale; they defied arrest and threatened the lives of good and honest citizens who were watching them, until numbers became too great for them to longer resist; they made their boast of revenge, and now I ask you, are the people to submit to this? What chance have they with such men as this?"

Kanapsa/Federhen's defense of the lynching and the legacy of his involvement deserves a thoughtful analysis. He defended the mob action in hanging without a trial two men, variously named Felix Constant, Constance or Constanes (later also named Coutray) and Edward or James or "French Mac" MacDonald or McDonald.

Kanapsa wrote: "Much as I deprecate lynching, I believe that I only speak the sentiment of every honest citizen in the territory when I say that these people have done right. I do not believe in the promiscuous hanging that was done here last summer, but this is the first attempt that horse thieves have made to gain a foothold and carry on their nefarious business in this section of the country.

"The people here are exposed to the Indians and the danger of these gangs of horse thieves coming from the north with stolen stock and them stealing others here and going back with them, and in the absence of proper legal protection, I believe they are right in making this first case an example which will so terrorize such characters as to prevent any further trouble of this kind, at least until the law becomes powerful enough to protect those who are willing to abide by its decrees.

"Some may say that these men are now dead and unable to answer the charges I make against them. To such I would say that I have not called these men horse thieves and murderers without being able to prove the facts.

"Undoubtedly there has been a large amount of lynching done in this territory, more probably than there should have been; but there is only one way to stop it, and that is, to so thoroughly and stringently enforce the law against these desperadoes that honest citizens will have some confidence in it, and not enforce it so weakly that the criminal has all the advantage, while the law-abiding loses all confidence in it and its protection to life and property.

"There is too much leniency to criminals; a little harshly enforced punishment would give honorable people more confidence and protection and make criminals less daring. Kanapsa."

The correspondent never wrote another word about the incident, but there were consequences.

On April 15, 1885, the River Press wrote: "Wholesale arrests. Deputy Sheriff Finnegan arrived from Birch and Dupuyer creeks Monday with eight prisoners supposed to have been implicated in the hanging of horse thieves on Birch Creek, a few days ago. Their names are James Wilson, Lew Mumper, John Morgan, Dick King, Kelly, Shindler, Finnerty and Mason. Sheriff James McDevitt will return in a day or two with a lot more, probably."

A second article read: "Preliminary examination. The examination of the parties arrested for implication in the lynching of McDonald and Constance was commenced this afternoon before Judge Chas. L. Spencer and will probably take up considerable time. The River Press will give the evidence as full as possible and when both sides of the story are heard, more intelligent conclusions can be arrived at. One of the parties implicated, at least, has given up what he knows about the affair, and some interesting revelations are promised."

On April 29 the news reported that Chouteau County District Judge Spencer gave lengthy instructions to a grand jury. He stated: "The alleged lynching of two persons in this county should command your consideration. I have been informed that two men were recently lynched, murdered in this county, and I wish to say there can be no greater offense against society, against civilization than this.

"We live under a government of law and should look to it for protection. Any encroachment upon the sovereignty of the law — taking the law into one's own hands — is a crime no matter what the parties may be guilty of. Even if the party or parties be red-handed murderers, there is no justification for such an act. Any man or body of men connected with this affair should be indicted. Our civilization cannot long endure if such practices are permitted to go unpunished. It is your duty to diligently inquire into the case. ... This is one of the greatest and most outrageous violations of the law that ever occurred in the county and should be treated accordingly."

The Chouteau County sheriff arrested eight, later changed to nine, men implicated in the Birch Creek lynchings.

A couple of hours after hearing the evidence, the grand jury reported "no true bill" on the charge of complicity in the lynching of Felix Constant and Edward McDonald on Birch Creek. The prisoners were given their liberty at once, and the River Press reporter added, "This ought to be a lesson to committing magistrates."

A May 28 Great Falls newspaper article had an interview with F.S. Stimson, manager for the Northwest Ranch Co. in Canada, who opined, "Some recently elected deputy sheriffs in Montana are raising a howl about it, but the general opinion is that as far as stock interests were concerned, the hanging was a great success."

Dupuyer resident Kanapsa/Federhen continued to defend citizens taking action in the alleged absence of law. He said there are only two ways to prevent stealing of stock, use soldiers to prevent any such outbreaks or just tell the settlers to take care of themselves. "If we cannot be protected, let us protect ourselves," he wrote in his weekly column.

Federhen had reported details about the lynching, but

he made no further mention of it. He was not arrested with the other suspects as far as the record shows. His column, formerly headlined "Birch Creek Breezes," was changed to "Dupuyer Dots" in 1886. The Birch Creek community had depopulated after September 1885, when Indian trader Joseph Kipp abandoned his store at Birch Creek and moved his goods to the Blackfeet Agency.

Only a few residents including Chas. Thomas, the proprietor of the saloon, and C.L. Bristol, the landlord, held down the fort at Birch. Another loss occurred in June 1886 when Henry Robert, pronounced Robarre, died at age 78, having been a Birch Creek resident for eight years.

Federhen's view that the law was no help against horse stealing was partially vindicated when in April 1887 two white men, William Aughey and James Francis, were arrested for stealing a mule and a horse belonging to an Indian named Bull Shoe. The suspects were released for lack of evidence by the local justice of the peace, but they were re-arrested, tried and acquitted in the U.S. Court in Helena.

The notorious lynching incident was not forgotten. A Dec. 3, 1887, report on the region in a Great Falls newspaper stated, "Leaving Dupuyer and passing through Birch Creek, the country becomes more hilly and less heavily timbered. Right beyond Birch Creek there stands a gnarled and withered tree, which was the scene of a 'lynching bee' some few years ago. Its knotted branches stand out in bold relief, and one cannot help shuddering as the tale is told of how two horse thieves met summary death. It is a gruesome looking tree, and a fitting place for such a deed as took place."

Army veteran Federhen, 32, moved in 1884 to Dupuyer, where he was employed as clerk and bookkeeper of J.W. McKnight and others. He started writing a column for the River Press in February 1885, but his writings tapered off after 1887. The Dupuyer Acantha wrote about his business enterprises and his musical talent after the newspaper's debut in March 1894. News items about him continued until his death in 1916.

The Birch Creek incident would come up again decades later in two accounts by local residents who implicated Federhen as one of the lynching masterminds, a difficult pill to swallow after reading the newspaper accounts of his many talents and accomplishments.

Federhen could sing and play a guitar and banjo, talents sought after on the frontier. In April 1889 the Choteau Calumet newspaper reported that he was a scenic artist. "He is engaged in painting an original design, which will soon add to the attractions of the Republican Headquarters Saloon on Main Street. The picture is creditable to the artist, and the owner's preference for local talent is very commendable. Federhen is open to engagements for paintings of any design," the news stated.

He decorated the bar in the Dupuyer Exchange with oil paintings and he volunteered to teach "voice culture and the rudiments of music" to the Dupuyer school children one hour a week.

By 1894 he was the secretary for the Republican Club of Dupuyer and Robare and after Teton County was created in 1893, he resurrected his pen name, Kanapsa, to support the effort to designate Helena for the permanent state capital instead of Anaconda.

A year later in early 1895 he announced that he had invented a new washing and polishing material, "far superior to Sapolio as a polishing agent for washing dishes, scrubbing floors, cleaning glass, etc." He called the washing soap, "Nox Em All." He made the soap with material from a clay deposit found on Sheep Creek and he was ready to market it, the news said.

He recorded a placer claim on the creek to secure his rights to the clay deposit, formed a co-partnership with W.H. Gallagher, renamed his product, "Alkazine," and then, a blow — he announced that "owing to an error in the placer-claim filing and some other complications, F.H. Federhen & Co. have given up manufacturing the polish."

In June 1896, the Teton County Commissioners appointed Federhen a justice of the peace for Dupuyer. The Dupuyer Acantha noted, "The judge is a new beginner, but is rapidly getting his hand in, and will prove a terror to persons who disregard the laws." His first stint in government was short-lived when he got into a snit with the commissioners. "He had requested a copy of the codes and as they are not forthcoming, he has decided to quit," the Acantha reported.

He continued his oil painting, producing mountain scenes at times, and he played at many musical engagements around the region while he ran for the office of justice of the peace in October 1896. He added house painting to his skills and he advertised that he purchased McKnight's typewriter and was open for "engagements for the execution of all sorts of typewritten work."

Federhen was elected JP of Dupuyer, but for some unstated reason, he failed to qualify in March 1897, so he took on the job of agent for the Massachusetts Benefit Life Insurance Association where he was "now ready to transact business in that line."

In April 1897 he started getting an Army pension of $6 per month, and whatever was his disability, he remained busy. He started selling a patented churn, introduced to the public with the following ad: "If you are thinking of buying a churn, it will pay you to wait a few days until I receive my sample of the best churn ever put on the market. Guaranteed to make butter from milk fresh from the cow in one minute."

By August 1897, Federhen was an agent for "useful and patented articles" including door checks, (a neat little device for holding doors ajar) and sash locks, the enterprise churn, a convex hone and strop and an indestructible wire basket.

He ordered a complete photographing outfit from the east, and in a week or 10 days was set to be ready for business.

By January 1899, he had joined McKnight in the old Dupuyer Acantha building to start a new business to sell real estate, make loans, and write fire and life insurance policies.

He earned a patent on land located two miles northeast of Dupuyer and in March 1899 he was again appointed justice of the peace for Dupuyer Township to fill a vacancy. He pursued the letter of the law with gusto.

In June the Dupuyer Acantha reported, "This morning in Justice Federhen's court Alfred Holi was fined $25 and costs for disturbing the peace and using obscene language on the streets. Being unable to pay the fine, the prisoner will be taken to the county seat to serve out his sentence. We are glad to see the authorities propose putting a stop to the disgraceful practice of using indecent language on the public streets and hope that the example in this case will be a lesson to others."

He was fond of doling out 60 days in jail in Choteau, the county seat. The building still houses the cramped jail cells today, although they are only used for storage now.

The incident with the Birch Creek horse thieves that happened in 1885, when Federhen was new to the area, cropped up again in April 1900, when the Acantha headlined a short article, "Blood-stained dagger."

"Among his collection of curios, Chief French of the fire

department of Great Falls has the dagger carried by Felix Coutray in 1885 together with 'French Mac' McDonald, a short mention of which appeared in yesterday's Standard. The weapon is supposed to have been instrumental in finding the vitals of more than one man during the time it was owned by Coutray.

"It is of the one-edged dagger pattern with an eight-inch blade, sharp as a razor, and a deer-horn handle. In the handle are inserted a pliers and small steel pick, and the scabbard is brass-tipped and made for wearing inside the pants belt.

"The dagger was taken from Coutray just previous to his hanging, and was given to Major Reuben Allen, at the time agent of the Blackfeet. The party's name who gave it to him does not appear as he was probably one of the lynching party and preferred to make the gift incog. When Major Allen left the reservation, he gave the dagger to Billy Jackson, the famous scout, who was the sole survivor of the Custer massacre, and whose death was reported in the Standard a few months ago. Jackson afterward gave the weapon to Chief French, who keeps it as a souvenir of Scout Jackson, and also of the last illegal hanging in what is now the bounds of Chouteau [Teton] County."

Federhen settled into a bachelor's life, making money on occasion from the sale of original songs, oil-painted artwork and gold, silver and nickel plating. He served off and on as a justice of the peace and acting coroner, led the services at the Methodist church in the absence of the Methodist minister and on some occasions dealt with horse thieves.

In March 1907 Frank Gallagher was charged with having stolen several colts belonging to F.D. Kingsbury of Dupuyer. Federhen dismissed the case because the prosecution failed to produce evidence sufficient to bind the prisoner over to the district court. Gallagher was at once re-arrested on a charge of mutilating brands, and was released on a $500 bond.

Pending a trial, Gallagher was again arrested for having a gelding in his possession that was not his own. According to the stock inspectors and county officials, Gallagher had been under suspicion for several months. They hoped the practice of horse stealing in the county's northern end would be "broken up for all time," the now Choteau Acantha reported. (It moved from Dupuyer in 1904.)

In June 1907 Gallagher pled guilty, was fined $100 and given 50 days in jail. But that summer he escaped, the date is uncertain, no newspaper account could be found, and apparently made his way to Canada. News came when he was recaptured in February 1908 in Fernie, British Columbia. However, "a great deal of red tape" was involved in his extradition, the Acantha said. Montana Gov. Joseph K. Toole declined to extradite him and Gallagher was let go. His wife joined him in Fernie.

In December 1908, Federhen was appointed U.S. Commissioner at Dupuyer, a post that involved hearing land disputes from homesteaders seeking land patents. His distinguished service was noted when he died, but years later people tainted his memory with accounts of his alleged role in the mob action at Birch Creek.

Federhen's career as an inventor, songwriter, businessman and public servant came to an end after a serious illness.

Of the two obituaries that were published, the July 7, 1916, Choteau Montanan's longer one read, "Frank H. Federhen, a well known old-time resident of the Dupuyer country, died at the McGregor hospital in this city last Tuesday morning after an illness of several years' duration. He had been troubled with locomotor ataxia, Bright's disease of the kidneys and other ailments, and it is surprising that he had survived as long as he did. He was 61 years of age at the time of his death, and was a native of Massachusetts. His parents, and brothers and sisters had long since passed into the great beyond — the only known relative now living being a cousin who resides near Boston.

"The deceased was a U.S. pensioner and at the time of the election riots in 1876 in New Orleans was a battalion sergeant major under General Brooke in the 3rd U.S. Infantry. He later came to Montana and after being mustered out of service, came to Dupuyer where he was employed as clerk and bookkeeper of J.W. McKnight and others. He had also served as local U.S. commissioner and justice of the peace at Dupuyer for a number of years, and was well known and highly esteemed by the people of that community. Funeral services were held in this city Wednesday afternoon under the direction of Rev. L.F. Haley of the Episcopal Church, and interment was made in the Choteau cemetery."

For all his entrepreneurial skills, Federhen died a poor man — his $33.33 hospital bill and his $48 burial were paid from the Teton County Poor Fund.

Years later came the allegations that he participated in the 1885 Birch Creek hangings of Felix Constant and Ed McDonald.

Author Helen B. West wrote about Federhen's alleged role in the Summer 1965 issue of "Montana: The Magazine of Western History."

West was the archives assistant at the Museum of the Plains Indian in Browning. Her 14-page account, "Robare: Elusive Outpost in Blackfeet Country," memorialized the pioneer community that was wiped out in June 1964 when Swift Dam, holding back the waters of Birch Creek, burst during the region's historic flood. She included first-person accounts in her segment on the Birch Creek hangings.

West said that the March 25, 1885, incident was an "explicit example of the vigilante syndrome." She quoted from Federhen's published account of the hangings but she misspelled Federhen's name as "Fetterhan."

She said Bill Jones named Federhen as the mob leader. Jones (in a manuscript) said he was present at the hanging. He was a well-known citizen who lived in the area and who died in 1934.

West said the informants recounted the incident with "detachment and dispassion." Jones said a young man was with the two horse thieves — a fact not mentioned in any newspaper accounts. Informant accounts of what happened to the third man differ, West said.

Jones said Federhen shot the young man, put the nooses around the other two men's necks, spit in their faces and cursed, "Die hard, you such and such." Jones said Federhen regretted his part in "forgetting himself" and was sorry all the rest of his life.

Jones said incorrectly that Federhen died in his thirties. West opined that Federhen must have had psychotic tendencies and informant Dorothy Floerchinger of Conrad (who owned Jones's manuscript) remembered his death as being at his Dupuyer cabin about 1913, also incorrect.

Finally, there's Bill Hall's story in the 1977 Dupuyer Centennial Book as further evidence of a Jekyll and Hyde personality. You be the judge. He wrote, "Federhen was known as the 'Hanging Judge,' although he did perform many marriages of the old settlers. ... My mother, Josephine Hall, witnessed the hanging on Birch Creek quite by accident. She often walked from our home, where Broesders now reside, to Robare for a few groceries and to visit friends along the way. About a mile from home she saw a group of people gathered by a large tree. She arrived there just in time to see Judge Federhen swing on the legs of one of the hanged men.

"It has been said by many old-timers that the judge's hair turned gray overnight and that he had the shakes the rest of his life. He kept his light burning all night — the dark gives one too much time to think," Hall wrote.

— 2 —

War on Wolves

November 7, 14, 2018

Montana offered the first statewide bounty on wolves in 1884, and the first Choteau newspaper report on the "terrible scourge of the range" was in December 1885.

"The cattlemen along the Marias and Teton rivers are becoming seriously alarmed at the great increase and extensive depredations of wolves and coyotes, and it is proposed to raise a fund by subscription for the immediate extermination of these pests. A number of men are now employed in poisoning carcasses, but owing to mild weather the result has not been satisfactory.

"Considering the high price of skins and the territorial bounty, wolf poisoning ought to furnish profitable employment to a large number of men, after the first heavy snowfall and severe frost, but with the additional bounty which will probably soon be offered by the stockmen, wolves should become as scarce as buffalo before spring.

"The following are the boundaries of the country, which the proposed bounty will cover: From the head of Birch Creek, near the Piegan agency, down the Marias to Baker's Battle Ground; thence to the mouth of Flat Coulee, on the Teton; thence up the Teton to Sun River Crossing; thence to the North and South forks of Sun River, the road marking the line; up the North Fork along the base of the mountains to the starting point at the head of Birch Creek," the Choteau Calumet reported.

Six months later, the newspaper offered a suggestion.

"The loss of calves and weak cows from ravages of wolves, mountain lions and other wild animals of Montana, is quite large every year — much larger than an unobserving person would imagine — and the necessity of killing out these wild animals and ridding the range of the expense of supporting them is every day more apparent.

"Now, while the round-ups are in progress, is the very time to get in effective work in their destruction. Each outfit should be provided with ample quantities of poison, and every scrap of meat left at an abandoned camp, the entrails of every beef killed, the testicles of every calf castrated, should be filled with a deadly drug, for no sooner is a camp abandoned or a piece of fresh meat left on the prairie than every present coyote is ready to slink from his hiding place and ravenously devour the refuse left.

"Wolves naturally follow in the wake of the roundup and every poisoned piece of meat left behind is almost sure to reduce the number of wolves on the ranges at least once. Let everyone scatter poison, and next spring we will have fewer wolves and more live calves."

By July 1886, the increase of calves was estimated at 30 percent greater than the previous year, "which is due principally to the systematic efforts that have been made to rid the ranges of wolves," the news stated.

Cattleowners supplied teams of men with provisions, bait and poison, "and it is probable that wolves have already ceased to be a serious impediment to the cattle and sheep industries. About 1,000 wolves were poisoned and their destruction is worth $10,000 to the sheep and cattlemen," the report stated.

"Wolves are still troublesome on the ranges in spite of the most determined and expensive efforts to reduce their numbers," the Choteau Calumet reported in March 1887.

"It is remarkable that some 15 years ago, when wolves

were not near so numerous as hostile Indians and there were no cattle in the country to speak of, about every other white man in this county was a professional wolfer and made money by poisoning wolves and selling the skins to Benton merchants at two dollars each. The occupation was then attended with the greatest hardships and dangers, but it was followed for years by hundreds of men until nearly all the wolves were killed off. It does seem that wolfing would now be as profitable as ever. With none of the former risks, with an unlimited demand and higher prices for skins, it should at least pay good wages."

The wolves adapted. A March 1888 report noted, with some hyperbole, "If it is true that wolves will no longer take poisoned bait, it is probably because they have learned to slaughter their own beef. They find that range cattle are much easier to bring down than the buffalo were. Mat Munroe, the well known ranchman, asserts that the wolves up his way not only slaughter their own beef, but round up small bunches of cattle, cut out the young calves and yearlings, drive them into the mountains and corral them for winter."

Two months later, the Calumet reported, "The ST and TL have been successful with their staghounds in exterminating the wolves in the vicinity of the ranches, but they have not been extensively tried yet on the ranges. Perhaps killing wolves near home is about the extent of their usefulness. They require rest after a few runs and would probably soon be used up on the ranges. Wallace Taylor recently had three valuable staghounds poisoned by old wolf bait set out two years ago."

Stockgrowers in the region banded together to form the Northern Stock Protective Association in November 1892, a few months before Teton County was created in March 1893.

The stockmen were C. Wallace Taylor, Walter S. Clark, Julius Hirshberg, Thos. Smith, Jno. Ward, F.W. Redding, C.W. Cooper, J.F. Burd, A.B. McDonald, Wm. M. Wright, Wm. Hodgskiss and others.

The object of the group was "the extermination of wolves and coyotes in a territory described as: beginning at the narrow gauge railroad crossing of the Marias, following up that stream to the mouth of Birch Creek, thence up that stream to the summit of the mountains, thence along said summit to the North Fork of Sun River, thence down said stream to Conch ranch, thence east to the narrow gauge railroad, thence along the road to the place of beginning."

The group's laws and rules included the formation of a 17-member committee that issued permits to members and that had a duty to certify that the animals for which an applicant desired to receive the bounty were killed within the boundaries. The reward was $3.25 for each wolf or coyote killed, the trapper or wolfer to retain the skins.

Any person putting out poison within three miles of any winter ranch of a member without permission was denied the bounty benefits, but the rule did not apply when animals were caught by trapping.

The Montana Stockgrowers Association recognized the "wolf problem" in April 1894 at its 10th annual conference. The members debated whether to increase the state's bounty money by special subscription or by a voluntary assessment on range holdings, but a different option won out — wolfers were to be employed on wages during six months of each year beginning in June.

The debate concerned whether a man on wages would work at wolfing honestly.

"Resolved that the members ... employ a man in each roundup during the months of June, July, August, September, October and November as a wolf poisoner employed exclusively to poison wolves, a salary and expenses to be prorated among the stockmen in the roundup district." Each district had a committee of three to select men to do the work.

"Something had to be done and the association has done something," the news reported.

A December 1938 recap of the 1894 wolf war stated, "The coordination of efforts on the part of the stockmen throughout the state brought about in the immediately subsequent seasons the gradual extermination of the terrible scourge of the range — the wolves."

Montana Fish, Wildlife and Parks noted that self-sustaining breeding pairs of the gray wolf probably became extinct in Montana by the 1930s. The U.S. Fish and Wildlife Service listed the northern Rocky Mountain wolf subspecies as "endangered" in 1973. Canadian wolves colonized Glacier National Park in 1979 and, according to FWP, now at least 30 breeding pairs populate the northern Rockies.

From the thousands that once roamed the plains following the bison, the gray wolf population is now about 550 animals mostly roaming the northwestern Montana forests. Hunting and trapping are allowed again, but baiting with poison is prohibited.

The Winter of 1886-87

February 17, 24, and March 2, 2016

Among Western lore the winter of 1886-87 has been labeled a "pivot point of a way of life never to be seen again," and, thanks to the Choteau Calumet newspaper published at the time, we can discern the local impact that the terrible winter had on the cattle industry that was based on "open range" grazing.

Promoting Choteau and its potential began with the publication of the little hamlet's first newspaper, the Choteau Calumet, on Dec. 18, 1885.

Just as the Choteau Acantha has an unusual name, the Choteau Publishing Co. adopted "calumet," defined as a Native American long-stemmed, ornamented tobacco pipe used on ceremonial occasions as a token of peace.

The Choteau Publishing Co. included stockholders, Pres. A.B. Hamilton, Vice President W.R. Ralston, Secretary E.C. Garrett, Treasurer Dr. Ernst Crutcher, and board members William H. Buck, Jacob Schmidt, Jas. W. Armstrong, S.C. Burd and Ed. Dennis.

Buck was the Calumet's editor while Ralston, Armstrong, Burd and Dennis were among the many cattle, horse and sheep stockmen who controlled the open range, meaning the unfenced expanse of grazing land from the Sun River to the Marias River, from the mountain foothills to the Missouri River.

By 1885, herds numbering in the tens of thousands had brought prosperity and eastern capital to the region from corporations investing in herds. Nowhere was the promotion of good times ahead better described than in the Calumet.

"John Smith, superintendent of D.A.G. Floweree's cattle herd, arrived from Dupuyer Creek on Sunday evening and left for Sun River on Monday. Mr. Smith states that the snow has almost disappeared from the ranges and the cattle are in the finest possible condition," said the Dec. 18, 1885, edition.

"Make a note of it. As an evidence of the resources of this section we have obtained the following statistics, which, though only a partial list of the livestock grazing within a radius of 20 miles of this place, will manifest, in a measure, the prospects of Choteau as a trade center: cattle, 30,400; horses, 3,975; sheep, 76,200; and swine, 246."

"Tourists sojourning in Montana for health and recreation should not fail to visit Choteau before leaving the territory. The main range of the Rockies, which is really some 40 miles distant, appears almost within a stone's throw of town, affording the most attractive scenery, cooling the breezes from the Pacific Coast during the summer months, and moderating the temperature while the severe blasts of winter prevail.

"All the creeks and streams which flow past the townsite of Choteau abound with trout, pike and other mountain fish, while chickens, geese and game animals, such as antelope, deer, elk, bear and mountain sheep, afford unlimited recreation to the sportsman.

"The climate is at all times conducive to health and vigor and is not considered unfavorable to invalids or convalescents even in the severest months of winter. To those desiring to combine business with pleasure, Choteau and vicinity offers exceptional inducements.

"The leading industries of the territory, mining

excepted, are to a great extent centered here, the country being remarkably favorable to agriculture, sheep and cattle raising; and parties seeking investment or desiring to become familiar with the management of stock can obtain all needed information and will find many opportunities for profitable use of capital.

"A large scope of country, wholly undeveloped, although believed to contain extensive mineral resources, offers attractive inducement to the prospector and miner, while the coal beds, water power facilities and wool and cattle products will in the near future command the attention of railroad corporations. Altogether this mountain country is the most naturally favored spot in all Montana," the Calumet said.

All was not Eden, however, and the Calumet on occasion reported bad news, but mostly the editor minimized the setbacks, starting with the winter of 1885-86, continuing through the dry summer and finally the devastating winter of 1886-87.

Buck described a severe snowstorm that occurred on Jan. 14, 1886, but he added that it was "much needed by the cattle and has come in time to prevent much suffering if not actual loss among the animals."

He then noted that it was reported that the cattle along the Teton were suffering for water. The river was frozen over and the snowfall had been very light in the valley. He said, "One man has been sent to cut holes in the ice, but the ice cutting should be done more extensively at those points where the largest bands of cattle are congregated."

A chinook arrived during the last week of January 1886 and Buck's screed that defended the cattle industry overshadowed reports of cattle still suffering on dry, overgrazed range.

He noted that the beef price was about as high as it

could go, and the range country was now virtually full of cattle, a good thing because no new ranges would be supplied with breeding herds. ... "Ranges that are properly stocked should and will appreciate in value slowly because the range area is gradually becoming less and will continue to diminish as the agriculturists make encroachments. There will be a range of country, however, for many years for the reasons that large portions of the territory are useless for all purposes save grazing. The business will move on, cattle and grass will grow as of yore, the people will eat beef and those who are in a position to furnish that commodity will thrive."

Leading up to the cattle-killing winter of 1886-87, the Choteau Calumet newspaper published a column by Bill Nye that, on the one hand, waxed effusively about the "wonderful growth of the great cattle growing and grazing industry," and on the other, provided a warning to the users of the open range.

In February 1886, Nye wrote, "So many millionaires have been made with 'free grass' and the early-rising automatic branding-iron, that every man in the United States who has a cow that can stand the journey seems to be about to take her west and embark in the business as a cattle king.

"But let me warn the amateur cowman that in the great grazing regions it takes a great many acres of thin grass to maintain the adult steer in affluence for 12 months, and the great pastures at the base of the mountains are being pretty well tested. Moreover, I believe that these great conventions of cattlemen, where free grass and easily acquired fortunes are materially advertised, will tend to overstock the ranges at last and founder the goose that now lays the golden egg."

The region had light snowfall that winter, and everyone hoped for "heavy and long-continued spring rains." By

April, there were prairie fires in the northern regions, but storms put them out and new grass was expected to result.

Although the summer heat was excessive, with the Calumet reporting, "and the wonder is that every hoof of cattle in the country has not been cooked a la barbecue," the first roundup in late July was completed one month earlier than the previous year, owing partly to fine weather, but mostly to the outfits using a more systematic gathering.

Two outfits separated at the Dry Forks of the Marias, with one part under the leadership of C.W. Taylor who went down the Teton, and the other under George Barron who took in the Marias range.

Calumet Editor Buck, ever the optimist, wrote, "Mr. Barron informs us that the grass on the ranges was never in better condition for cattle, and unless next winter should be unusually severe, with deep snow, there is not likely to be more than the average losses."

Noting the dry hot weather at July's end, Buck remained optimistic, "There is time enough yet for new grass to grow and 'cure' before frost sets in, but there is some danger that late rains will keep the grass green until the frost kills it. It has been a remarkable season, so far, but it may redeem itself long before cold weather arrives."

At that time there were a reported 70,000 head of cattle were on the Teton and Marias ranges and in September another roundup occurred. The best authorities stated that the beef cattle were in prime condition and only cows with sucking calves looked poor.

It snowed the second week of September 1886, and with it came a respite from the dry weather. "We were blessed with a refreshing rain yesterday, and this morning Mother Earth was clothed in a lovely mantle of snow. To the delight of cattlemen and ranchmen, the long looked for has come, but we fear a little too late for any good."

Frank Higgins and Sam Mitchell, with their "C2" beef herd, Higgins were enroute to the Northern Pacific for shipment. Other herds were being driven to Maple Creek for shipment via the Canadian Pacific. The ranges were very dry and water scarce, the Calumet said. The Floweree herd of about 3,000 head was enroute from the Yellowstone, with plans to winter between Birch and Dupuyer creeks.

Buck noted that the prairie fires had done some damage, but he believed the beef to be in unusually fine condition based on the branding reports, and, "These fortunate features will probably compensate for exceptional losses, should they occur, from scarcity of feed and water."

The worst of winter started with a cold snap in January 1887, "just long enough to see the old year out and the new year in, but was broken by a chinook early Sunday morning and the thermometer went up above the freezing point. The mild spell only lasted until Tuesday evening when the wind changed to a northeaster, accompanied by more snow, which rapidly developed into a first-class blizzard, lasting until about two o'clock the following morning. Since then the weather has been stormy, but not extremely cold, the mercury rarely falling below the cipher."

What was discovered later, was that slush froze into an impermeable crust wherein cattle could not feed. Winter came on in earnest, when cattle, sheep and horses covered the open range in all directions around the small hamlet of Choteau.

Sheep rancher Ralston had his flock break away, but herder Ed Welch brought in all but 40 or 50 head, after remaining with them all night in the storm.

"Talk about shipwrecked mariners and snowbound travelers, there are not many tales of peril by sea or land that will size up with this instance of courage, endurance and devotion to duty. Mr. Ralston informs us that the ranches being well provided with hay and shelter, there is no reason to anticipate heavy losses even if the remainder of the winter should be unusually severe," Calumet Editor Buck wrote.

On Jan. 15, Buck reported, "The weather for the past week has been principally Chinook, but the mercury has not wandered far above the freezing point and the snow has not materially decreased. High winds, however, have collected the snow into drifts, leaving a good portion of the ranges free for grazing."

On Jan. 29, he said, "The weather during the past week has been mild, the mercury ranging between five degrees above and five below the freezing point. High winds from the west and southwest blew continuously day and night and at times with great violence, but last evening about five o'clock the wind changed to the northwest, a heavy snowstorm set in from that quarter and within three hours the mercury fell from 30 above to 20 below zero, remaining near the latter point until daybreak this morning. It continued snowing throughout the night and today, and there is no indication of fair weather as we go to press. The mercury is 12 degrees below zero, a light wind blowing from the northwest.

"Continued inquiries regarding the condition of sheep receive but one reply. They are doing well enough. Cattle are reported poor, but on their feet and rustling," Buck reported.

By March 12, Buck had received reports that the storms had taken a toll, but he refused to believe that the terrible winter would change the West.

He wrote, "Every possible effort was made to relieve the cattle in this neighborhood. Riders were out when the mercury was at its lowest and the wind so fierce that it seemed impossible for any living thing to face it. Losses can hardly be estimated yet, but one of our leading stockmen, who prefaced his statement with the remark that the public should not be misled in this matter, believes that not less than 25 percent will be the average loss throughout the county. Many of the cattle are certainly dead and more are in good shape to follow, but 25 percent will doubtless cover all losses even if the present month should prove unfavorable."

Buck was aware, however, that reports were circulated back East that large numbers of dead cattle were being found piled up in coulees and live animals were skeletons. He said it was just a wild story.

On March 19, he announced, "Reports from the vicinity of Great Falls state that 30 percent is the present estimate of cattle losses, while sheep have lost 20 percent." Still, he added, "We are unable to understand all this palaver about the losses of the past winter causing a revolution in the present system of stock-raising.

"For 13 or 14 years stock-raising has proved a most profitable industry. ... Large fortunes have been made by the present system of cattle growing," he said, "and no material change should be deemed necessary. ... The time has not yet come to abandon the industry or for corralling and feeding stock in winter, as some pilgrim writers would have us believe."

In July, Buck reported that ranchers shipped to Fort Benton 7,810 hides from cattle that succumbed to the winter at Dupuyer, Choteau, Fort Conrad, Birch Creek and Piegan. He said the losses ranged from 25 to 35 percent of the herd from the Teton, Marias and Sun river ranges. It had finally dawned on Buck and the ranchers that they took tremendous risks in placing cattle on the plains without feed. That month, the U.S. Department of Agriculture listed the total cattle losses of the United States in the 1886-87 winter at 2,086,030 head.

From then on, the Calumet sported advertisements for "agricultural implements of every description including Champion reapers, Champion mowers, Tiger hay rakes, and Diedrick hay presses."

Buck also changed. "Now that grass is everywhere abundant, those who have use for hay should not fail to put up enough to last through two or even three winters. Experienced farmers know that hay when properly cared for will keep well and retain its nutrients through three winters, and they also know that those who fail to take advantage of a good grass year usually get left the year following," he said.

Choteau area cattle king Jesse Taylor in a July 1887 interview said, "The cattle business is undergoing a change for which myself and others have prepared. The large ranges are breaking up here as well as elsewhere, but this will always be a great cattle country and our people will adapt themselves readily to the new conditions." The era of open range was done, and the age of range management had arrived.

— 4 —

Zachary T. Burton, Irrigation Promoter

November 18, December 2 and 9, 2015

For the mover and shaker that he was, Zachary Taylor Burton should have had more than five small mentions in the 1988 Teton County history book, but his forgotten contribution will be uncovered in this tale on his life and times.

Z.T. Burton, as he was known, first came into prominence in Helena when he became the "Receiver" in the U.S. Land Office in February 1884. An active Republican, Burton had a short stint on the Helena school board and he tried his hand at being a deputy sheriff for three months in 1886. After that he entered a law partnership with R.H. Howey specializing in contested land claims, titles and "conveyancing." He was admitted to the Montana bar in August 1886.

A sketch of his background was published as part of his next foray into public life, when he sought the nomination from the Republican Central Committee for probate judge of Lewis and Clark County.

"Born and brought up on a farm in Indiana, he thoroughly understands and appreciates the wants of every grade of the laboring class. When a boy, by the labor of his own hands, he provided the necessary means of educating himself, his father having been disabled by rebel bullets while leading a company of soldiers to storm the Confederate works at Vicksburg. Mr. Burton spent three years under the eminent educator and author, Dr. H.L. Wayland, at

Franklin College, Indiana," a Burton advocate wrote in the Helena Weekly Herald in September 1886.

"He afterwards studied law and was graduated, at the head of his class, in the law department from the Indiana State University in 1878, after which he practiced his profession for several years in his native state. Mr. Burton came to Montana with his family in 1882. He sought and obtained employment as a clerk in the U.S. Land Office at Helena, in which capacity he worked for little over a year, when his abilities were duly recognized by his superiors at Washington and he was appointed Receiver of said office. He occupied this position but a short time when he was removed by President Cleveland for the sole reason that he is a Republican," the newspaper said.

Burton was only 34 years of age, but the promoter said he was "one of the best accountants in the Territory."

He was not nominated, but became active in Helena city politics, and continued to rise to a position of prominence in the Republican Party. He joined a new law firm and had as a client, the Northern Pacific Railroad, while being elected as the captain of the Grand Lodge of Sons of Veterans in Helena. He appeared on behalf of contestants in high profile land cases in 1887, 1888 and 1889, while raising a family with his wife Henrietta, "Rettie," as she was known, and children, Addie, Glendora and A. Wolf Burton, "Wolf" being Rettie's maiden name.

Z.T. Burton is first mentioned in a Choteau newspaper in May 1890. The Montanian profiled the Eldorado Ditch Co., first, then wrote, "Burton & Allen of Helena have taken up a large tract of land under the desert land laws on the bench some three or four miles north of town. They are also taking out a ditch expecting to store water in a large reservoir. They intend to make this the model horse ranch of the state and we think they will, as they expect to spend over

$50,000 in fitting it up."

In August 1890, Burton, J.P. Bouscaren, C.W. Burton, U.G. Allen, L.H. Hershfield, P.H. Leslie and W.M.G. Settle filed articles of incorporation of the Eureka Reservoir Canal and Irrigation Co. The capital stock was $200,000 divided into 40,000 shares of $5 each. Helena was named as the principal place of business.

The Great Falls Semi-weekly Tribune mentioned the new venture on Sept. 24, 1890, in its Spray of the Falls column. "Z.T. Burton of Helena has been up near Choteau where he is interested in the Eureka canal and a large area of desert lands. With irrigation these lands will become a source of great profit."

Likewise in February 1891, the Montanian said, "Next week will witness the beginning of one of the most important enterprises which has ever originated in northern Montana. Mr. Bouscaren, chief engineer of the Eureka Reservoir Canal and Irrigation Co., is now in Helena in the interest of the company, and will soon advertise for bids for the construction of the canal work to begin about the 1st of April. He expects to send out a party next Monday or Tuesday to finish the surveys. This canal will reclaim an immense body of our finest blue joint hay land."

The funds for the construction of the big reservoir and canal were in the treasury of the company, and the bill for the formation of the new Teton County, to be carved from Chouteau County, was in the hands of the legislative committee on towns and counties, thanks in part to Burton's machinations.

Burton and his family moved from Helena in October 1891 into their spacious residence they called "Ivy Lake" on his namesake bench along the Eureka Canal he developed five miles northeast of Choteau.

"It is pronounced the finest country residence in

Chouteau County," the newspaper said.

C.F. Green & Co. had completed all their work on the Eureka Canal in the fall of 1891 except the deep cut at the reservoir, which was about half done. "The main canal is finished and water will soon be turned in from the Teton River by means of a side cut which comes in below the reservoir. Mr. Angus Bruce is finishing up the lower end of the canal this week," the Choteau Montanian reported.

Another article said the ditch represented an investment of about $40,000 and nearly 200 men had started work on June 1, 1891.

A May 1892 newspaper published a glowing account, "Z.T. Burton is one of the progressive men of the upper country, and has done much during his stay in that section to bring about its fullest development, being the president of and one of the moving factors in the Eureka irrigation company."

Three months later, Burton filed 20 final proofs on desert land embracing more than 6,000 acres of fine bench lands within a few miles of Choteau.

In January 1893, a few months before the Legislature created Teton County, Burton, and four others filed the articles of incorporation of the Montana Land and Water Co. The capital stock was $1 million.

After that, Burton repeatedly traveled to St. Paul, Minnesota, to meet with representatives of various colonies of farmers to entice them to relocate in northern Montana.

Hollanders came first, but Burton sought Mennonites to come too. He scheduled $25-round-trip monthly excursion trains from St. Paul to Great Falls and he advertised in 18 state papers about the undeveloped wealth of northern Montana.

"I receive about 250 letters a week written in Scandinavian, German and other foreign languages, as well as in

English, and the labor of translating and answering these letters is no small job," Burton told a reporter in Great Falls.

By December 1894, the Choteau school census was 139 in the district, with 23 children on the Burton Bench, up from two the previous year.

The paper reported, "Settlers are constantly arriving on the Burton Bench, east of town. Twas only Wednesday we noticed an outfit from Minnesota pulling through town for their new home on the bench. There were two young men, a two-horse wagonload of goods and two cows in the procession. They had come on the railroad to Great Falls and thence by the wagon road to Choteau. The women are to come through by rail to Collins as soon as the men get the house made ready for them."

For all his efforts to portray the Burton Bench as some kind of bountiful Eden, Burton could not shield his colonists from the extreme weather during their first winter.

A particularly strong storm hit the region in February 1895, when the temperature went from 40 above with a west wind to a north wind "carrying a snowy mist with it cold enough to freeze a Laplander." The temperature dropped to eight below in only a few hours.

Six to eight inches of snow fell throughout the next day and when the storm ended it was 26 below zero, the coldest of the season.

The first weather-related casualty on the bench occurred less than a month later during a second storm. "Peter Anderson, 73, a rancher living on the Burton Bench east of town, was in Choteau last Saturday during the blizzard. While here he became somewhat intoxicated, and about 5 p.m. he and a fellow rancher by the name of Joseph Darling started for home on foot. Darling tried to dissuade Anderson from going, but could not. On Sunday afternoon Henry Steiman, while out riding, discovered the body of Anderson about three miles from Choteau lying in the road."

The news report said Anderson was a man of some means from Sweden. His son in Minnesota had planned to join him in the spring.

Life seemed good for Burton as he enthusiastically developed an expansive irrigation system northeast of Choteau in the 1890s. If things had worked out, his legacy would have been assured in the annals of the county.

Alas, it was not to be. By the autumn of 1894 Burton's company, the Montana Land and Water Co., had $80,000 in capital paid in but $100,000 in debt. He had hoped to get an estimated 219 farmers to take up 160-acre tracts but it was slow going.

All was not rosy for the farmers either. In November 1895 L.T. Morgan, who was doing the threshing for the farmers of the Burton colony, said that the yield was large enough but that most of the grain was shriveled on account of early frost. Water was kept on the land too late in the summer by reason of the desire to raise a full crop. The spring had been late and growth of grain was backward. The farmers made the mistake of taking chances on a late fall.

Then too, stockmen were complaining bitterly about the condition of fences on the Burton Bench. They said that loose barbed wire was scattered in all directions and was very dangerous to stock. "Allowing fences to lapse into such a condition is a strict violation of the law and owners become liable to prosecution," the Montanian wrote. The roads in the area were quagmires when it rained.

Burton's dream, or scheme, some said, began to crumble when Syracuse University filed a complaint for foreclosure in August 1896 against Z.T. Burton and his wife, Rettie, their company, and creditors including the Kansas Loan and Trust Co. that had funded the canal and land development. Newspaper research did not reveal why the university held a $5,000 promissory note that was in default.

Added to its debt woes, the Montana Land and Water Co. was fighting a water-rights lawsuit against the Farmers Cooperative Canal Co. that had been incorporated in 1897. It offered a better deal in how it provided water than did Burton.

The Burtons continued in business while the foreclosure proceedings dragged on. Rettie Burton became the Burton postmistress. Their three children grew up and married.

In January 1899, while they were away, a fire that started in daughter Addie's photographic darkroom, destroyed their beautiful home on the bench along with nearly all of their household goods, clothing, provisions, the company books, and about $100 worth of post office supplies. The insurance policy had recently expired and was not renewed.

In March, the farmers petitioned for the establishment of a post office in place of the discontinued Burton office. The new post office, called Farmington, was located at Munson's store, which was about 1.5 miles north of Burton.

The judgment of foreclosure was entered in March 1900 and a sheriff's sale of most of Burton's assets was ordered, although it did not occur until November 1901. As the new century began, Zachary, 48, and Rettie, 46, lost control of 1,200 acres of land and their remaining 2/6th interest in the irrigating ditch that diverted 3,000 miner's inches of water from the Teton River into the canal system.

Something happened in early 1901, the newspapers never said, but Burton left the state and headed to Indian Territory (now Oklahoma.) Rettie got a divorce in September on the grounds of nonsupport.

First the River Press of Fort Benton, and then the Montanian of Choteau wrote what seems to be the only negative reference to a now disgraced Burton, his business acumen and character.

"Z.T. Burton came into prominence in the upper Teton country a few years ago as a promoter of irrigating enterprises. He put in a large irrigating system on what is known as the 'Burton Bench,' a few miles north of Choteau.

"It is now a thickly settled farming community, and the residents have put in a cooperative canal, dispensing with the Burton system. ... He has lately turned up in the Indian Territory, where he was selected by the Chickasaw tribe as their local representative, to succeed his brother, who has been elected as U.S. senator from Kansas. Secretary of the Interior Hitchcock has, however, refused to confirm his appointment, after looking up Mr. Burton's antecedents. The position in question carries a large salary and calls for great legal ability."

— 5 —

Bachelors Club

March 9, 2016

Choteau newspaper editors had a penchant for light-hearted banter when they wrote about the bachelors' clubs of Choteau and Bynum, but the bachelor girls, the spinsters, not so much.

In March 1892, the Bachelors Club of Choteau advertised a masked ball at the Choteau House on St. Patrick's Day, March 17. "A general invitation is extended and a royal good time is anticipated. Come, everybody. Tickets: ball and supper, $3."

By Christmas 1895, the male singles' social scene was well established. "The ladies of Choteau don't like to be outdone, but they have concluded that an old maid's banquet could not be a success. The bachelors don't care, however, as they all agree that there is not, and shall not, be an old maid in the country."

Later, Montanian Editor S.M. Corson wrote, "The bachelors of Choteau banqueted on Christmas Eve at the Choteau House. No one can appreciate a good time like the average Teton County bachelor and in view of this fact and to insure conditions productive of the most possible comfort and freedom, no married men were allowed except the sheriff and 'mine host.'"

The puns regarding bachelors were a mainstay of newspaper copy from then on.

In March 1898, the Teton Chronicle published a comment by the Blackleaf special correspondent named, "A.

Leaflet," who said, "Blackleaf furnishes the following items of interest to bachelors: Girls are at a premium here and on the upper Muddy, but coyote pelts are accepted as full legal tender. No old maids are advertised, but good-looking school ma'ams don't last long. We make matches to order and pay the preacher in county bounty."

A week later a Burton Bench correspondent wrote, "One thing we lack here now is more women. I would like to see something hanging on the clotheslines besides old woolen shirts. I would like to hear the prattle of more small children, instead of the unearthly yell of some tomcat on the warpath. Quite a number of good honest girls could here find a good home and pretty good husbands. We have too many old bachelors for comfort. Nothing will thin our ranks but a war with Spain or an epidemic of matrimony."

On another page, the Chronicle noted, "The bachelors of the Bynum Social Club, as the boys have styled themselves, have completed arrangements for a free dance at the Town Hall in Choteau next Monday evening. Not only members of the club are invited, but everybody who wishes to attend. The boys being unable to entertain the members of the club at any time during the winter, take this means of repaying those who entertained the club at their homes."

Bachelors had a special status it seems, based on this entry in September 1901. Whether it was tongue in cheek is hard to tell. "Ord Aynsley was called up to Choteau on the jury but was excused by Judge Smith he being a bachelor and had his dough made when called from home and had to get back at once to bake bread."

Six years later in March 1907, the clubs were still going strong. "On Friday, the bachelors of the little 'cow town' of Bynum gave their annual banquet and dance. All the cowpunchers for 20 miles around were in attendance. The boys met at seven o'clock and called the roll, and they found there were only two missing out of the 30 members. On inquiries being made, it was learned that one of them had strayed off his range and got mavericked by a pretty school ma'am; the other missing member, so rumor said, was in Helena trying to rope in somebody's hired girl."

And a year after that, the Elizabeth correspondent wrote, "The annual banquet of the bachelors in this district was celebrated at John C. Salmond's ranch on Deep Creek on Saturday evening, Feb. 8, 1908. The night was spent with cards, checkers and other games, also recitations and music. Refreshments were served at midnight and everybody had a real good time. The members left for their home the next day with pleasant smiles on their faces and were cautioned to be on the watch during leap year so that all the members present at this banquet can be at the next."

In "Reflections of a Bachelor," a regular column, the writer offered this quip: The Maiden asked, "Of the men of your acquaintance who have married, which do you think are the happiest?" The bachelor replied, "The dead."

— 6 —
Stock Stealing
December 21, 28, 2016

Cattle and horse stealing and illegal branding occurred as soon as the stock was put out on the open range in north-central Montana, and trials for those crimes occupied the first cases in newly formed Teton County in 1893.

A rancher and his cowhand working the Marias River range were among the first on the new docket, according to the Oct. 13, 1893, Montanian newspaper. "Sheriff A.B. Hamilton yesterday took Jim Johnson and Fred Brazil, the two men charged with illegally branding a lot of colts, to Great Falls, where he will place them in jail for safe keeping, pending the completion of the Teton County jail and their trial at the next term of court. ... After the return of Sheriff Hamilton from the pursuit of the train robbers on the reservation last week, that vigilant officer with his deputies made a dash north to the Marias and brought in Johnson and Brazil, who were charged with branding colts not belonging to them.

"It is represented that Johnson and others have been for some years engaged in the horse business with more success than what their stock would warrant," wrote Editor S.M. Corson.

John W. Tattan and W.G. Downing appeared at the instance of the Board of Stock Commissioners to assist Teton County Attorney James Sulgrove in the prosecution. Two of Great Falls's leading attorneys, James Donovan and M.M. Lyter appeared for the defense.

On Dec. 1, Corson wrote that the case occupied almost the entire day and the hour being late, court adjourned until the usual hour the next day. The state called five witnesses and the defense called two witnesses with the third testimony coming from Johnson himself.

"After supper, counsel on both sides occupied the time in argument until 11 o'clock when the jury retired and remained out until nearly two o'clock when they returned a verdict of not guilty and the court dismissed the accused, and ordered Brazil released next morning."

Corson added his opinion under "Notes: Donovan and Lyter made an excellent defense in the Johnson case. Tattan and Downing, who conducted the state's side of the case, did poorly, not bringing out their evidence as they could have done."

It was a bit of a blow for Teton County's first attorney Sulgrove when Judge Dudley DuBose closed the third term with the numbers showing that none of the six criminal cases on the docket resulted in convictions. The county had been organized the previous March and the able judge dealt with 46 cases, six criminal and 40 civil, with only three civil cases to hold over to the next term.

Corson softened his tone on Dec. 8, with the words, "The county attorney had carefully prepared the case which was ably presented and conducted, and failure to convict was due entirely to the failure of the prosecuting witness to substantiate his complaint. Ex-Senator Downing made a powerful plea as did also Mr. Tattan, but the meat was not in the kernel."

The River Press in Fort Benton shed light on the stock stealing issues when on Dec. 20, 1893, it published a letter from Chinook rancher A.H. Reser, who took issue with the harsh penalty of one year in the penitentiary for illegal branding. He asked stockmen to consider a change in the law. "Had we not better stand on an equal footing with other industries and punish cattle thieves according to the value of the animal? It's our duty to repeal the law as it now stands," Reser wrote.

The Press stated, "It is a fact that it is harder to convict a person of illegal branding than of almost any other crime, and this for the reason that it is hard to convince a jury that branding a $15 calf or a $30 cow is deserving of a year's imprisonment. When one considers how easy it is for illegal branding to be carried out upon a large scale, and how difficult it is for the stock owner to recover his property or even prevent the theft, the punishment does not seem so great; but it is generally one particular animal for which the accused is tried, and as Mr. Reser says, the law is made too strong — the jury considers the penalty too severe, hence convictions are very few in number."

The jury acquitted James A. Johnson of grand larceny for stealing horses and his partner in the alleged crime, Fred Brazil, was then released.

Corson noted before the trial, "There were five men in the county jail this week, viz: Johnson and Brazil on trial for horse stealing; Mart Brunnel, undergoing a sentence for selling whiskey without a license; Wm. Mead, sentenced for forgery, and Wm. Haffron, charged with burglary. All these men are in a jail not 16 feet square. Too bad the new jail is not ready."

By January 1894, the law had found several new suspects in the stock stealing business. The first was Charles Fenty (sometimes printed as Finty) of Choteau who was arrested in Great Falls for cattle stealing.

"About a week ago Fenty engaged John Mestis to assist him in driving eight head of beef steers to Great Falls, promising to pay $20 for such services. They arrived at the Falls on Saturday and Fenty offered the steers to C.N. Dickinson at an outrageously low figure, so low in fact that the latter's suspicions were aroused. Calling in Stock Inspector Sam Heron, who was in the city, an examination of the brands was made and it was decided to place Fenty under arrest. The cattle bore the brands of J.C. Adams, Geo. Quail, Sam Ford and Frank Truchot."

Fenty proclaimed his innocence at first, but in March he pleaded guilty and was sentenced to three years in the penitentiary. Frank Shannon was charged with illegal branding of John Horn's colt in February, but he was found not guilty.

Then James Parker who had been wanted by the authorities in Choteau for some months for implication in a certain illegal horse deal, was brought in from his home on the Marias River and put in jail.

This time, when the March 1894 term of court started, Teton County Attorney Sulgrove's zero conviction rate from 1893 was behind him and the odds turned in his favor.

The first case to come up was that of Jack Hackland who was charged with grand larceny by having stolen a 999-branded cow and selling it to Wm. Hodgskiss. The jury brought in a verdict of guilty and fixed the penalty at one year in the penitentiary and a $100 fine.

On March 23, Parker's trial for stealing colts became a bigger victory than even Sulgrove anticipated.

"This case was related to that of James Johnson, who was tried for a like offense at the December term, but was acquitted. In this case the witness, Brazil, who had worked for both Johnson and Parker at the time of the stealing, turned state's evidence and detailed the manner of procedure in the branding of stock, whereupon Johnson, who was in town as a witness, was arrested upon a charge of feloniously branding stock." Parker was found guilty.

"At 1:30 p.m. this afternoon Johnson and Parker were

brought into court, Parker to receive sentence, and Johnson to answer to the charge which had been filed against him, and to which he pleaded guilty."

Before he sentenced them to three years in Deer Lodge, Judge DuBose in open court went on an extraordinary tirade directed at Johnson about how the law would always prevail. Corson faithfully transcribed it for the Montanian readers.

The March 28, 1894, River Press wrote, "A week of splendid work. Last week marked a revolution — a field day in Teton County, in the conviction of some half a dozen cattle thieves. ... The action in Choteau last week will be a wholesome check on cattle stealing for a time, and will also rid the upper Marias of the gang who brought a stigma upon that section."

Corson wrote on March 23, that Hackland, Geo. Morris, Haffron, Parker, Johnson and Fenty would that night have the distinction of being the first occupants of the new county jail. Sheriff Hamilton escorted them the next day to Deer Lodge where they were expected to put in a combined sentence of 22 years.

Alas, not exactly. The Board of Pardons granted Hackland a "diminution of sentence" in January 1895, Johnson and Parker the same in July 1896 and Fenty in August.

Elizabeth Collins, The Cattle Queen of Montana

August 2, 9, 2017

In the lexicon of the Old West, the title, "Cattle Queen of Montana," is nearly as familiar as "Wild Bill Cody."

It was the title of a 1954 American Western movie starring Barbara Stanwyck and Ronald Reagan, but the movie's plot line had nothing in common with the real "queen," Teton County rancher Elizabeth Smith Collins.

Elizabeth or "Libby" became the Cattle Queen of Montana at age 47 in 1891. During a prolonged illness in the winter of 1893-94, she wrote down her life experiences and a newspaperman, Charles Wallace, in 1894 compiled and published the harrowing tales of her early life, including how she was crowned that name. She then became an entertaining lecturer throughout the East and West extolling the virtues of cowboys, ranchers and Montana, in general, even as she tried her hand at mining along McDonald Creek, in present day Glacier National Park.

Her remarkable story as told in her riveting book will take some time to tell.

In August 1879 Libby and her husband, Nathaniel, drove their cattle herd from a leased ranch in the Prickly Pear Canyon to the Teton River valley in the vicinity of present-day Choteau.

By then the U.S. government had shifted the boundary of the Blackfeet Reservation from the Sun River to Birch

Creek and the valley was opened to settlement. A small population of mixed-blood people lived around the old vacated grounds of the Blackfeet Agency, (about three miles north of present-day Choteau) but its neighbors, white traders A.B. Hamilton and I.S. Hazlett had big plans.

They moved their trading post to the spot where the Hirshberg building is now located in Choteau, Hazlett filed the plat for the new town, and invited cattle ranchers, businessmen, settlers and cowboys to see what the 15-mile-long Teton Valley had to offer.

Elizabeth Collins would later write that when she moved to Old Agency, (it was renamed "Choteau" on Aug. 29, 1883, when the town plat was filed at the Chouteau County courthouse in Fort Benton) it had but 500 souls, with a single store and one or two houses. The Collinses put their cattle herd on the open range in the lush valley, and they set up a homestead at a point midway up the valley and some one-half to three-fourths of a mile from present-day Choteau.

Their only child, a daughter Carrie, was born in November 1881. She is credited with being the first white child to claim Choteau as a birthplace.

The couple had been married in Helena by the pastor of the Methodist E. Church on Dec. 31, 1874, when Libby was 30 and Nat was 42. They had met two years earlier, when Nat was in Silver City, 12 miles from Helena, operating a placer mine using hydraulics and sluice boxes. Libby was then a camp cook for 18 miners at Canyon Creek.

Nat Collins had been well known in the Helena area, but his name, and the name of "Mrs. Nat Collins," as was the formal custom of the time, did not start regularly appearing in the local newspapers until 1886 when the Choteau Calumet newspaper began operations. By 1888, they were frequently mentioned in the River Press in Fort Benton, the county newspaper of record until Teton County was created in 1893. The Great Falls Tribune also noted the Collinses' comings and goings.

In 1886, needing more range, the Collinses changed their location to Willow Creek. They also had a hay ranch at Hay Coulee, one and a half miles away. They retained a house in Choteau, 24 miles away, where they lived during winter when Carrie attended school.

Hamilton, who was the county assessor, reported in the Calumet in June 1888, "Nat Collins has a fine band of stock and dairy cattle grazing near his residence, all fat and frisky. Among them I noticed a number of valuable three- and four-year old beef steers that would command ready sale and high prices in any market. Mrs. Collins is the same hospitable lady who formerly resided near Choteau, and I can vouch for the fact that her cooking has lost none of its former universally acknowledged excellence."

Some of the 180 head of cattle that they bought with the proceeds from selling the Silver City mine had died in two harsh winters in the Prickly Pear Canyon, but the cattle that were left multiplied.

Elizabeth Smith Collins was first dubbed the "Cattle Queen of Montana" in the Oct. 23, 1891, Montanian newspaper published in Choteau.

It read in part, "A Cattle Queen. Mrs. Nat Collins, of Choteau, has earned for herself the distinction of being the first lady in Montana to raise, ship and accompany a bunch of beef steers to the Chicago markets. On Wednesday she returned from a successful trip east with two carloads of cattle and one of horses, which she sold at good figures — the cattle to Chicago and the horses at Sycamore, Iowa."

To understand how and why Collins at age 47 had the temerity to undertake the solo journey traveling in the caboose of a cattle train with her male counterparts, we have to turn to her life experiences. Thanks to her autobiography published in the fall of 1894, we can do just that.

Born in 1844 in Rockford, Illinois, Libby Smith was one of many children of Solomon and Elizabeth Woods Smith. The family moved to Iowa when Libby was 10, and they stayed there for at least six years. Solomon, who turned 59 in 1860, got "gold fever" and the family headed to Denver by wagon train. It took six weeks and on the way Libby had her first encounter with Indians.

An Indian approached the perky teenage and tried to kiss her and she slapped him, she related, which was witnessed by his father, the chief.

Libby had no formal schooling, but her memory of events made it easy for her and St. Paul newspaperman Wallace to write in her book some remarkable anecdotes about life on the frontier.

Solomon was not content to stay in Denver and followed a gold lead to Port Pueblo, and on the way Libby had encounters with a mountain lion and a black bear. She shot a mountain lion that was attacking a man. The gold mine was a fraud and the family went back to Denver, where her father got "lung fever" and died. Besides that, Indians killed one of her brothers.

With another brother and her mother both sick, Libby, to make ends meet, became a caretaker for two motherless children at Central City for $40 a month.

When the unnamed brother got "calico fever," he and their mother went back to Iowa where he married. Libby stayed behind and learned to make embroidered buckskin gloves, which she sold at $10 a pair.

She witnessed murders and described mines in Central City, then went back to Denver when the brother arrived with his new bride. Libby wrote that she did not like her sister-in-law, and jumped at the chance to go with her brother on a visit to Pike's Peak, 100 miles away. Another encounter with Indians followed, in which Libby was wounded. Then she got "brain fever" but recovered. Her mother pleaded with her to go back to the "states."

Her adventures continued when her brother got a job on a wagon train and Libby tagged along following her mother's wish. Her trip was interrupted by an Indian attack, and this time she was captured, and her brother was presumed killed. It is unclear what her age was at the time.

Luck was on her side because the attackers included the chief who she had met a few years earlier, and instead of being treated harshly, her plucky slap had impressed the chief, and she became his daughter's companion.

Collins's book described in detail the horror and torture dealt to the other captured people, words that are difficult to read. The book became a sensation when it was published, and for good reason.

Although normal for the time, the words Libby used to describe the Indians are not appropriate for use in this tale, as she detailed her six months with them. She was released when members of the Denver militia entered the camp, and the chief allowed her to leave.

She lost her hair after another bout of fever, and when she returned to Denver, she found her brother alive and her sister-in-law so kind and helpful to the temporarily bald, vulnerable Libby that Libby changed her mind about disliking her. That chapter of her life ended when a flood destroyed their cabin on Cherry Creek, and her life as a wagon train cook began.

— 8 —

Elizabeth Collins, From Trail Cook to Miner and Rancher

August 16, 23, 2017

Teton County pioneer Elizabeth "Libby" Smith, who in later life would become the "Cattle Queen of Montana," decided to follow her brother's lead and take a job with the Denver-based Overland Stage and Freighting Co.

Smith was still barely out of her teens, when she became a cook for the company's wagon trains, the only female in a party of 160 men accompanying 100 wagons drawn by six teams each. Overland freighted from the Missouri River to points in the Rocky Mountains.

She adapted to working in the company of those men, and would later write that they worked together with mutual respect.

She wrote, "I have lived all my life among those reputed to be rough, uncivilized and uncouth, but I defy the world to produce a class of people who as a rule are more endowed with true, noble and praiseworthy qualities of manliness; who will more quickly aid in righting a wrong; who will more gallantly espouse the cause of a slandered woman, or who will more willingly extend a helping hand to a brother in need and misfortune, than the sturdy pioneers of the far west."

Her autobiography, written in 1894, included stories of her 12 round trips traveling to Omaha, Nebraska, her promotion to scout, the wagon train's encounter with a

sandstorm, when a bison chased her and a lengthy description of geysers in what would become Yellowstone National
Park in 1872.

With winter approaching in which snow stopped all
freighting, Libby and her unnamed, unmarried brother,
flush with cash from their employment, decided to stay
in Virginia City, Montana. Misfortune visited them again
when the brother got "brain fever" and they exhausted
their funds. The enterprising Libby then rented a sewing
machine for $7 per month and sewed clothes for people.
She garnered a contract for producing flour sacks at five
cents each and she could sew 100 in a day and evening, net-
ting $5 per day.

But prices escalated without new food stocks coming
into the snowbound city from Salt Lake City. As her brother
recovered, Libby would go from cabin to cabin and cook for
the miners to make ends meet. The gold rush in Montana
was well underway, having started in 1862.

As Libby gained cooking skills, she also witnessed the
work of vigilantes, which she wrote about. Her knack for
finding employment remained strong and she nursed a
young miner to a point that he could travel, and she accompanied him to St. Louis, the first time she was on a train
that the two boarded in Salt Lake City. By the time she got
back to Montana, her brother had gotten discouraged and
had left for Denver, and Libby was alone again.

Libby's book has detailed descriptions of placer mining
and of cattle ranching, but getting back to her journey to
the title of "Cattle Queen," and ranching in Teton County,
we find her alone in Bannack. For a year she was a house-
keeper and a nurse for a "respectable lady" and at the same
time earned $25 a week working as a nurse for a "leading
physician in Helena."

She saved a tidy sum of money. Her savings were in her

room where she boarded, and a major fire consumed many houses including the one where she lived. "My savings was taken from me" ... and everything she owned with it.

Penniless, she went to Silver City, 12 miles away, to stay with friends. She found work as a cook again, for 18 miners in Canyon Creek and earned $75 per month. On New Year's Eve, 1874, in Helena, she married Nathaniel Collins, whom she had known about two years. He owned a placer mine at Silver City near where she was employed. He was 37, Libby was 30.

"We prospered and were happy," she wrote.

On Nov. 19, 1875, Nat's leg got tangled in a rope tied to a colt he was attempting to saddle-break, and his leg became "badly bruised and terribly shattered." Libby somehow got Nat into bed, but when she went to the creek to retrieve some water, she slipped on the steep bank, badly sprained her left foot, and shattered and splintered some bones. She crept on hands and knees to the cabin, where they both lay with no heat or food for two days and two nights before rescue came.

The Columbian newspaper in Columbia Falls wrote a review of Elizabeth Collins's book, "The Cattle Queen of Montana," on Jan. 31, 1895.

"Montana's Cattle Queen. Mrs. Collins has been captured by Indians and led an adventurous life. One of the conspicuous exhibits in the Montana building of the World's Fair was a life-size picture of Mrs. Nat Collins, who has been known far and wide throughout the West for a number of years as 'The Cattle Queen of Montana.' The story of Mrs. Collins's half century of life reads like a dime novel. ...

"She is now a rich woman, and thousands of cattle bear the Collins brand. There is hardly a phase of rough life on the frontier that she is not familiar with. In the early days in Montana the only law was the law of Judge Lynch, and Mrs.

Collins has seen many rough characters swung into eternity by the ready hands of vigilantes. She has also tried her hand at mining and has taken part in seven rushes to new diggings. Despite her manlike life, she is still very much of a woman, and many a sick cowboy has been nursed back to health by Aunty Collins," the newspaper stated.

To continue the tale, in November 1875 Nat and Libby were both severely injured and unable to light a fire or prepare food at their cabin located beside a placer mine outside of Silver City. The reference to a dime novel above was apt; the couple lay there "half famished, half frozen" for two days and nights, until Old John rescued them. He was Chinese and the book quotes his broken English phrases of surprise.

Nat and Libby recovered in the hospital in Helena, finally going back to the cabin in May 1876. The illnesses had cost them $1,500, and then the dam failed at their reservoir above their mine, wrecking their expensive sluice boxes, valued between $800 and $1,000.

They sold their mine holdings in August and decided to go into the cattle business. By November 1877 they had purchased 180 head and were situated on a rented ranch in the Prickly Pear valley eight miles from their former home.

They lost cattle that winter, and lost more cattle the next winter, after which Nat decided in the spring of 1879 to look "for a more favored locality" and found the Teton River valley.

Nat's injury and subsequent illnesses and frailty would plague him the rest of his long life, so much so that he was granted a pension as an invalid in November 1892, based on his service in the U.S. Army for three months in 1861. It would be the direct reason why Libby traveled with the cattle instead of Nat on that fateful train trip in 1891, but her experiences had prepared her for supposed hardships.

They delayed moving to the Teton River valley over the summer of 1879 while Nat recovered from illness in the Helena hospital, but they completed the move on Aug. 3, 1879, when Choteau was called Old Agency. The valley had been the home of the Blackfeet Agency until 1876, when the reservation boundary moved to Birch Creek and the lands from the Sun River to Birch Creek were opened for settlement.

They located at a point midway up the Teton River valley about one half to three-fourths of a mile from present-day Choteau.

The last chapter of Libby's book describes the valley in 1879 as having a single store and one or two houses. Their daughter Carrie was born in November 1881, the first white child to claim Choteau as a birthplace. The white men who were already living in the valley had Indian wives, including the two founders of Choteau, Al Hamilton and Isaac Hazlett. Libby said she did not talk to a white woman for a year.

She described the horrific murders of Mrs. Armstrong and Mr. Morgan and the illegal hanging of the suspect and her taking in of the two children that Mrs. Armstrong had cared for. She noted the death of esteemed Choteau physician, Herbert Smith, both incidents becoming important chapters in Choteau's history.

In 1886, needing more range, the Collinses changed their home ranch location to Willow Creek and established a hay ranch at Hay Coulee, one and a half miles away. Their herd with its "77" brand multiplied.

— 9 —

Elizabeth Collins,
Pioneer Cattle Rancher

August 30 and September 6, 2017

Cattle ranchers Nat and Elizabeth Collins prospered in the Teton River valley and on its tributary, Willow Creek, during the 1880s and 1890s.

Elizabeth's book, "The Cattle Queen of Montana," says the couple arrived in the valley on Aug. 3, 1879, but the federal census shows them still located in the Prickly Pear valley on June 25, 1880. No matter, the old newspapers regularly reported on their doings starting on Nov. 24, 1881, with the announcement of the birth of their daughter, Carrie, at Old Agency, the original name for Choteau.

The Collins family moved their home ranch to Willow Creek in 1886, but they eventually set up a second home in Choteau, after Carrie started school.

Collins wrote in 1894, "The home of the writer is situated on Willow Creek, Teton County, Montana, 24 miles distant from Choteau. Day or night, rain or shine, storm or calm the latch-string is always to be found on the outer side of the doors, and within will be met a hearty, cordial and sincere welcome to all who honor the humble home with their presence, and so long as there remains upon the range a single hoof bearing the 77 brand, its owners will, if need be, willingly and cheerfully part with the same in order to share with their friends or those in need a crust of bread."

Nat Collins reported that he did not lose cattle in the

terrible winter of 1886-87, but he would have been one of the few who were spared. Elizabeth wrote that it was the custom to dispose of beeves to buyers who came to the ranch and bargained for them.

The story of her becoming the cattle queen began with, "This practice was quite general with the ranchmen, but, just in order to be contrary, I suppose — as all women have the general reputation of being — I at last expressed the opinion to my husband that we were not receiving full value for our stock by practicing this custom, and at last succeeded in inducing him to ship a consignment of beeves to the Chicago market. The experiment proved a most successful one and the following year found us, as fall approached, again preparing to ship to Chicago.

"All went well during the time of gathering and 'cutting out' the cattle destined for the long journey, but just a few days prior to the start for Great Falls, from which place the cattle were to go by train, Mr. Collins became quite sick and he dare not undertake the hardships of the trip, and thus there remained but two things to be done — either I must myself accompany the stock or the shipment must be abandoned, for it would be folly to trust to a stranger the handling of the beeves and the large amount of money received from their sale in Chicago.

"For a lady to undertake such a task and carry it through to a successful ending was an event as yet unheard of in the history of the cattle trade, but notwithstanding this fact, I determined to try — no one knows what they can do until they try — and therefore, when the time had come for the start, it found me ready, dressed and prepared to mount the 'grub wagon' and take my place in the procession with the lines by which the team was guided in my hands. The cowboys in charge of the stock were all well known to me and trustworthy men, and therefore I experienced no unusual anxiety as to the trip from the 'home ranch' to the shipping point, Great Falls, but beyond that I knew not what to expect.

"My greatest fear was of the 'railroad men.' I had always heard of them —much as eastern people hear of 'cowboys' — as a class utterly devoid of the slightest dictates of manly instinct; men who would insult, mistreat, rob, plunder and even cut the throat of a woman did she but dare to show her presence in the 'caboose' of their train; men who delighted in rowdyish acts, fought regularly before breakfast and after each meal, washed their hands and faces only upon the occasion of their marriage or the funeral of a relative."

After a four-days' journey, during which time they camped out wherever night overtook them, Collins, 47, and her wranglers with a cattle herd and a "band" of horses arrived at Great Falls.

Collins's October 1891 trip with the cattle to Chicago became a national news sensation, each story written with slight variations. Here is the version taken from her 1894 autobiography.

"I had previously ordered cars for the reception of the stock, but upon arriving there, was informed that I would be obliged to await the arrival of more stock for shipment, as my consignment was not of sufficient number to load a full train and, therefore, would not be shipped until such time as a sufficient number of cattle had arrived to constitute a full train of 22 cars, each containing 22 head of beeves.

"Another difficulty also arose. Among the rules of the railroad company, I was informed, was one in particular, which prohibited the granting of a pass to a lady who wished to accompany stock upon a cattle train, or even allowing her to ride upon such train provided she paid full fare. Here indeed was a dilemma. My stock was ready for shipment but I could not ship. Expenses were fast accumulating and everything was going wrong. Not only did I have cattle to ship, but, in addition, a 'band' of horses were to be sent east. Among these was a valuable pacer, which I had intended to place in the hands of an experienced trainer upon my arrival in the states, and which I had every reason to believe would at some future date return a handsome price.

"As I drove from the city to camp one morning, I found this animal lying at the outskirts of the camp, stone dead. Asking as to the manner of its death, I was informed that a cowboy had saddled the animal, preparatory to riding it and that, becoming frightened, it had reared and fallen backward and broken its neck. I have during my life passed through many a discouragement and have been overtaken by many a disheartening event, but, without exception, I never experienced a more trying time than during those 10 days of waiting before I finally saw my cattle and horses loaded and safely started on their long journey and found myself sitting bolt upright on the leather cushions of that hard-riding 'caboose' with the much-dreaded 'railroad men' about me.

"The accident to my highly-prized pacer for the time unnerved me, and leaving the camp, I wandered to the banks of the river nearby, and there, alone and unseen, gave vent to my disappointment and discouragement in tears and moans. But it does a woman good to cry, and when I had finished playing baby, I arose, with a determination to succeed or die, and on the banks of that muddy Missouri I vowed to secure my rights and accompany my stock to market, or, in an attempt to do so, forfeit each and every individual head of stock I owned in the effort to ascertain why I should be denied the privilege and right.

"With this determination firmly fixed in my heart I returned to camp, took my team and again drove to the city.

Meeting a representative of a Chicago commission firm, whose headquarters were at Great Falls, I told him of my situation and requested him to telegraph the proper officials of the railroad at St. Paul, stating the circumstances and requesting permission to travel with my stock. This he kindly consented to do, and as a reply, the local agent of the railway company received instructions to grant me a pass, and accompanying the same was a notice to all conductors and employees of the train upon which I was to travel to 'provide for the comfort of Mrs. Nat Collins, the bearer of this pass, in every possible way and treat her with all respect due a perfect lady, under penalty of discharge upon failure to do so.'

"At last the victory was won and from that time forward all went as merrily as a marriage bell. As the train stood at the station ready to start upon its long journey, upon the platform of the depot was gathered a large number of cowboys and ranchmen from various sections, who had arrived in the city with stock for shipment, and as I mounted the steps of the smoke-stained caboose, from that crowd of sturdy men arose a long and hearty cheer, and as the signal for departure was given, and amid the excitement of the moment as the cowboys waved high in the air their broad sombreros, in a clear voice rang out the words, 'Success to Aunty Collins, the Cattle Queen of Montana.'"

Elizabeth Collins Writes a Book

September 13, 2017

Teton County rancher Elizabeth "Libby" Collins gained national attention in October 1891, and for the next few years she accompanied her cattle on the train to Chicago.

In November 1892, the Montanian reported, "Choteau's Cattle Queen is receiving the attention of the press of the country since the publication in the Montanian of Mrs. Collins's trips east. Two articles have appeared in this paper giving accounts of her and of the way she conducts the sales of her livestock. Both of them were widely copied throughout the United States, so that today Mrs. Nat Collins, of Choteau, is known throughout the length and breadth of the land as 'The Cattle Queen of Montana.'"

In October 1893, she traveled with three cars of cattle. A Helena newspaper reported, "When Mrs. Collins left her hotel yesterday to take the train, she rode in an express wagon with a 'prod-pole' in one hand and a lunch basket in the other, the very embodiment of woman's rights. She is a large woman and has the appearance of being able to take her own part without any assistance from the sterner sex."

In June 1894, the Montanian reported that Collins returned after a three-months visit east. It read, "While at St. James, Minnesota, she was taken sick and remained there two months, during which time she wrote a complete history of her experiences in the West and which will shortly appear in form. While away, Mrs. Collins delivered four or five lectures on 'The West and Western Ways' which were well received by the people and drew immense crowds."

Having written the book and convinced of her knack for telling a good yarn, Collins, 50, began lecturing, charging 50 cents admission for adults and 25 cents for children.

In October 1894, the Montanian reported that Collins arranged with the Slayton Lyceum Bureau of Chicago for a lecturing tour of one year through the East. It said, "This is the same bureau that brought out and managed Susan B. Anthony, Katy Stanton, Belva Lockwood and other well-known women. Mrs. Collins's book will soon be issued. The lectures are to commence about Nov. 15 so we may not see the old lady again for a year."

"Mrs. Collins is an entertaining, but not elegant talker," an Indiana newspaper reported. "Her stories of Western life were very interesting and well told. She acknowledged her shortcomings in the use of elegant English and deplored the fact that she had never been permitted to attend school."

In January 1895 Collins hired Byron Corson of Choteau as her state agent for the book sales. "The Cattle Queen of Montana," sold for 50 cents plus eight cents to pay postage.

The Anaconda Standard printed this review: "She's Wild and Woolly. Verily Montana's cattle queen is a Lu Lu. ... Mrs. Collins claims to have passed through some pretty tough experiences while enduring the inconveniences of frontier life. These are fully set forth in tolerably good English and enlivened by numerous illustrations. This literary effort of the queen, while it may not become a classic, is bound to afford interest to the hordes of lovers of cheap literature and at the same time amuse those Montanans who have the temerity to look through its pages."

The Columbia Falls newspaper said, "The story of Mrs. Collins's half century of life reads like a dime novel."

In March 1895, Collins arrived home from her eastern trip. The Montanian reported, "She has been absent nearly six months, during which time she has visited as far east as Ohio. During her absence she delivered a number of lectures, and, but for ill health, would have continued in the lecture field for some time longer. As it was, she has been quite ill most of the time she has been away, and finally she was compelled to return to Montana on that account. Already she feels the good effects of the bracing mountain air and thinks that she will be able to comply with the request of numerous friends to publically address them one week from tomorrow, April 6. Mrs. Collins is an interesting talker, both on and off the platform, and there should be a large attendance on that occasion."

Not content to raise cattle, write a book and complete a lecture tour, Collins decided to renew her acquaintance with placer mining near Lake McDonald.

— 11 —
Elizabeth Collins Takes Up Mining
September 20, 27, October 4, 11, 2017

Montana's cattle queen, Elizabeth Collins, loved the country west of Choteau where she and her husband, Nathaniel, operated a cattle ranch in the 1890s, but she grew up in a Colorado mining district and married a placer mine operator in Helena, and a yearning to strike gold or some similar mineral never left her.

While an agent sold her autobiography for 50 cents per copy, and with her cattle in good hands, Collins arranged lectures on both sides of the Continental Divide. It was while in Kalispell, most likely, that she learned of a copper strike.

The first mention of her mining interests was in June 1895 when the Choteau Montanian reported, "Mrs. Nat Collins arrived home Tuesday evening after a six-weeks' absence, three of which were spent at McDonald Lake in Flathead County, where she has some mining properties.

"Mrs. Collins went there on business and for rest and pleasure, in company with her brother Chandler Smith of Columbia Falls. ...

"She pronounces that section rich in mineral and destined to soon be one of the leading copper producers of the state. Also, that the timber there is sufficient to supply the needs of the state for years. In fact, she says the natural resources of the valley of the North Fork of the Flathead, at the head of which is McDonald Lake, are beyond anything she ever saw," the newspaper said.

The Dupuyer Acantha had reported on the strike in the Flathead in December 1894, although other versions were probably published. "New Copper Discoveries. William, familiarly known as Billy Jackson, an attache of the Blackfoot Indian agency, who stopped off here on his way to Helena, ... is exhibiting some very fine specimens of copper ore taken from a recent discovery in the Flathead country. Joe Brown and a fellow prospector by the name of Starks are said to be the parties who first ran across the lead. They struck it last July while following their calling.

"The croppings are said to extend several miles through a limestone and porphyry formation. Small shafts have been sunk on the lead at several points and the result in each case proved highly satisfactory to those who did the work. Jackson thinks the deposit of copper ore will on careful investigation be found to be something stupendous. He says another year will witness some rich discoveries in that section.

"Twenty-nine mineral locations have been made. The lead is situated a dozen or so miles south of McDonald's lake and almost directly across the main range from St. Mary's lake. It is in a very mountainous section of country, where the snow lasts three-quarters of the year. A pack trail is the only road connecting with the outside world. This, it is hoped, will be made into a fairly passable wagon trail next season. Mr. Jackson is very enthusiastic over the new copper country and feels confident it will witness a large amount of development next year," the Acantha said.

The Montanian reported, "Sam Lesuer returned on Tuesday from the McDonald Lake country where he has been looking over the much talked of mineral deposits. Sam says there is plenty of ore but that it will take millions to develop a paying thing out of the proposition. He says further that Mrs. Nat Collins, our 'cattle queen,' is making things lively over there as she does wherever she goes. She is now showing the ore deposits and mineral claims to some St. Paul capitalists with a view of interesting them in the matter."

By June 1895, Joe Kipp and partners had shipped in a large amount of supplies and were cutting a wagon road from Belton to the mines. "The movement of the Kipp syndicate is taken as an indication that earnest development work is to be carried on. There are large bodies of copper-silver ore that are easy to mine, and promise well," the Columbia Falls newspaper said.

By October, Collins was speaking in glowing terms of the gold prospect in the McDonald Lake country. In January 1896, the Acantha repeated what news it could gather about the riches in the Flathead, noting that M.F. Gleeson "reports having made a rich strike in some of the leads that are owned by Garrett and Kipp."

In 1901, Collins, Garrett and Kipp were still looking for a "wealth-producing proposition," but not before Collins, 51, and her brother, Chandler, 38, rowing to their claims, nearly drowned in Lake McDonald's cold, deep water.

As it was, a well-known prospector and miner with a dubious past, lost his life falling out of the same rowboat. The Montana newspaper reports varied and the reporters at the time misspelled the man's last name. This tale substitutes the correct one: Frank "Pony" McPartlan.

The first reports were short, but they were long on the truth. The Aug. 9, 1895, Great Falls Weekly Tribune wrote, "Parties just returned from the Lake McDonald country, report a fatal accident on the lovely lake, which is now eliciting so much interest on account of the beautiful scenery surrounding it. It seems that a party of three hunters and fishers were out on the lake in a rowboat, when a sudden storm came up on the evening of Aug. 5. One of them, a prospector and guide, named Frank McPartlan, formerly a resident of the Sweet Grass country, was drowned in the capsizing of the boat. The other two men reached the shore safely. So far the body of McPartlan has not been recovered."

The Anaconda Standard on Aug. 14 reported, "Mrs. Nat Collins, the cattle queen of Montana, was an occupant of a boat that capsized on Lake McDonald a few days ago. Mrs. Collins is a woman of marvelous nerve, and, realizing the dangerous situation, she quietly loosened her bloomers and other garments, and struck out for shore, riding the turbulent waters of the inland lake like a cork with a feathered sail."

The Dupuyer Acantha republished the Kalispell Interlake's version, "According to the report of the occurrence, McPartlan was in a boat with Mrs. Collins and Chan Smith and in some way the boat was upset. They were not far from the shore at the time, and McPartlan offered to assist Mrs. Collins to shore. He was not making much progress, and Smith caught Mrs. Collins and they clung to the boat. As soon as McPartlan released his hold of Mrs. Collins, he sank and did not come to the surface afterwards."

The Columbia Falls newspaper version reported, "The three were in a boat rowing from the hotel up to their camp, when by a sudden lurch or an attempt to change his position by McPartlan, the boat was capsized and the occupants thrown into the lake. McPartlan started to swim to shore, several hundred yards away, with Mrs. Collins, but he had not gone far when he sank to the bottom and was seen no more. Mr. Smith, who had clung to the upturned boat, managed to push it over to where Mrs. Collins was struggling, after McPartlan went down, and the lady's life was thus saved.

"Billy Elsmere and Mr. Abbott heard the screams when the boat capsized and they hastened to the rescue. Mrs. Collins and Mr. Smith were nearly exhausted, and the rescuers arrived in the nick of time.

"McPartlan's body had not been recovered at last accounts. The dead man was known in the mining districts of this section. He came here from the Sweet Grass and was working prospects at the head of McDonald Creek, where Jos. Kipp and his colleagues are located. He was known as a big hearted and generous man, but not an accumulator of money."

The River Press in Fort Benton reported, "By the upsetting of his canoe Frank McPartlan was drowned Monday afternoon near the head of McDonald Lake. He was paddling across the lake from the huckleberry patch two miles beyond the main inlet, pointing toward the new hotel. The breadth of water where the accident occurred is between two and three miles and very deep. McPartlan had prospected north of the lake to some extent and acted as a guide to parties up to the boundary line and beyond."

When Collins arrived back in Choteau, she provided a perfunctory explanation without any drama, of what happened.

"Mrs. Nat Collins arrived on today's coach from the McDonald Lake mines," the Aug. 16, 1895, Montanian reported. "She says Frank McPartland [Note: the correct spelling is McPartlan] was suffering from heart trouble and was dead before he struck the water, and that she kept the body afloat herself quite a long time before assistance reached her. Mrs. Collins is an example of what the 'new woman' would have you believe she is trying to be, but can't. The difference lies in the fact that Mrs. Collins does, while the 'new woman' professes to believe she does many useful things."

Strange to say, however, in January 1913 Collins's

brother, Chandler Smith, told the Columbia Falls newspaper, the following version:

"When asked for one incident that stood out in his memory more clearly than any other, he related an experience on Lake McDonald when Frank Patridge [sic McPartlan] was drowned. In company with his sister, Nate [sic Elizabeth] Collins, the 'cattle queen,' and Mr. Patridge, they were rowing a boat from the foot of Lake McDonald to the head where Mr. Smith and a sister were working on some mining claims. It was getting well on toward dusk as they reached the other end of the lake, but instead of landing, Patridge suggested that they stop rowing and rest from the long trip in the boat.

"They continued conversing for some time, when they discovered that the boat was drifting back from the shore a distance of perhaps a mile or two. Chan picked up the oars and started rowing. As he turned his head to look over his shoulder to get his directions, he felt the boat lurch and looked around just in time to see his sister and Patridge go out of the boat. As the boat turned back, he went out also, but clung to it and a second later succeeded on getting a hold of his sister. Patridge never came up.

"Clinging to the overturned boat they finally made themselves heard and were rescued by Billy Elsworth, who was camping at what is now the Glacier hotel place. The next day the lake was dynamited and every effort made to find Patridge's body but without success, and to this day, Chan is unable to account for the suicidal action of his traveling companion."

And then there is a disturbing retelling of McPartlan's drowning in, "Death & Survival in Glacier National Park: True Tales of Tragedy, Courage and Misadventure," by C. W. Guthrie and Ann & Dan Fagre, published by Farcountry Press, May 23, 2017.

Guthrie wrote that Glacier Park historian L.O. Vaught interviewed local residents who said that the three people, Collins, Smith and McPartlan were at Snyder's Hotel (where Lake McDonald Lodge stands today) "drinking and quarreling all day." They all climbed into a rowboat headed to McPartlan's cabin at the head of the lake.

Guthrie's story continued that McPartlan was in the prow, Smith was rowing and Collins was in the stern with a jug of whisky. A quarrel started when McPartlan wanted the jug and Smith would not hand it over, but McPartlan got up to get it and capsized the boat. Smith and Collins were holding onto the boat, but McPartlan was holding onto Collins' cloak to keep afloat because he was wearing a heavy gun and holster.

Guthrie wrote that Collins weighed around 300 pounds, and the cloak's chain was choking her. When she managed to unfasten it, the cloak and McPartlan went underwater.

In her narrative, Guthrie said the hotelier heard their cries for help and set out in a steamboat to rescue them. Supposedly, Collins was too heavy to pull up and they "tied a rope under her armpits" and towed her to safety.

One more version, a letter by Collins herself, described McPartlan's (spelled McPartland in later accounts) drowning in Lake McDonald.

On Aug. 23, 1895, the Montanian wrote: "Kipp, Montana. Aug. 8. Editor of the Montanian. According to promise, I now write you a short sketch of my trip to the mines during the past few weeks. I took the passenger train at Blackfoot, and after a very pleasant ride through magnificent scenery, I arrived at Belton, 'the foot of the lake,' where we are met by George Snyder, who is waiting for us with his little steamer to take us across the lake of 18 miles in length and four miles wide. When you look into the water and see the reflection there, one thinks that the heavens and earth have met.

"Peace and strength seem to be there. Here will be found quiet and rest for those who are in search of it, fine fishing for those who want to fish, and all kinds of game for those who like to lose themselves in the forest.

"Brother Chan [Smith] was waiting for us at the landing at the 'end of the trail,' with saddle horses and a camping outfit. We left next day for the mines, a trip of three days, which I found to be a very difficult undertaking. It was a very hard trip, as you must know, for the distance is only 28 miles. Upon reaching the mines we find snow, and sitting down to rest, we gather flowers with one hand and make snowballs with the other.

"Upon looking around I find some splendid looking quartz, and I am satisfied that here lies a grand mineral belt, but not what can be called 'a poor man's diggings,' on account of the transportation being so difficult and costly, and if any one goes in there, be sure and take your own blankets, provisions, saddle horse and pack horse, for then one can go and come where and when he pleases.

"There are three camps at work taking out good quartz, but it is so high up, the season will be short, and there will be plenty of snow.

"Upon our return to the lake we were accompanied by Frank McPartland, in whose death we feel we lost a true and faithful friend. Arriving at the lake, Chan, Frank, and myself, took a small rowboat and started for the camp at the head of the lake, Chan rowing. After a quarter of a mile from shore, Frank without any warning whatever, fell backwards into the lake. As he fell the weight of his body upset the boat, throwing us all into the water.

"As it went down I caught hold of Frank's coat collar and tried to hold him above water, and in fact, did swim with him quite a distance, till I reached the boat, which Chan was trying to upright. But before I could reach the boat, his weight had become too much for me, and he seemed to slip right out of my hands and he was gone. During this time he (Frank) never made a struggle, and in my opinion he was dead before he struck the water.

"Chan and I hung onto the boat and I screamed for help, which soon arrived, and we were saved while poor Frank has a watery grave. His loss is mourned by all and felt by his pardners. [sic] He was a true friend in time of need and was always throwing out sunshine through a smile, trying to lighten the burdens of others; was hopeful, kind and cheerful, many happy hours have the tired miners whiled away, sitting and listening to his playing on the banjo, and singing."

Collins then mentioned her disbelief that McPartlan could have been responsible for killing a man in 1886 in Sweet Grass Hills, a story that was added to the mention of his death in Montana newspapers, but no matter, he still got a mountain named after him, Mt. McPartland in Glacier National Park.

What version do you believe?

12

Frank McPartlan, Prospector

October 18, 2017

Cattle Queen Elizabeth Collins's friend and mining prospector Frank McPartlan, has a mountain named after him, "Mt. McPartland" in Glacier National Park.

He arrived in Montana in the early 1880s and the Mineral Argus was the first to mention him in connection with the mining strike in Maiden in present-day Fergus County.

When he died, his obituary in the River Press in Fort Benton highlighted his mining work, "He took part in many of the mining stampedes in Meagher, Fergus and Chouteau counties during the past 20 years, and was engaged in the same pursuit at the time of his death."

In the fall of 1879 he was one of a party who first discovered the mineral wealth of the Maiden district. The Collar mine was extensively boomed in 1882, and in that year Si Eaton of St. Paul and other capitalists, were induced to put up money for the enterprise. The newspaper wrote, "A mill was built at a cost of $125,000 and the first run proved that the boasted value of the lead was a myth. The moneyed men pulled out, part of the plant was bought and removed by P.W. McAdow, of the Spotted Horse, and the balance of it went to ruin. While the excitement lasted, McPartlan was regarded as a millionaire, and comported himself in a style becoming such a personage."

McPartlan was afterwards appointed justice of the peace for Maiden Township and is credited with performing the first marriage, but he was also known for being a

heavy drinker. "His judicial decisions were sometimes re-
garded as of doubtful legality," the Argus wrote.

"In 1885, McPartlan joined a party of prospectors who
made a rush for the Sweet Grass Hills, which were then
within the limits of the Blackfoot Reservation. They found
some pretty fair placers, and wintered in that vicinity. In
May 1886, McPartlan got into a dispute with Jno. Moy,
one of his partners, over the trivial matter of the size and
boundaries of Rhode Island, and the quarrel wound up with
McPartlan cutting and stabbing his opponent so seriously
as to cause death. McPartlan was arrested and lodged in the
Chouteau County jail ... ."

The River Press went astray in some of the facts in the
1895 obituary, but the story published in May 1886 began,
"Ben Short arrived in the city Tuesday last from the Sweet
Grass Hills, bringing a report of one of the most horrible
murders in the criminal annals of Montana, which took
place at that camp on the 10th. From what we can learn,
F.T. McPartlan and a man named Moley [note the different
spelling] became involved in a dispute in regard to Rhode
Island — its size, boundaries or something of the kind.

"Both hailed from that state and stoutly held to different views on the subject under discussion. Finally McPartlan drew an outline of the little state, and when Moley
questioned its accuracy, the former commenced the assault
with a knife, stabbing his victim in the neck, arms, breast
and abdomen. The stab in the neck severed the jugular vein,
and was sufficient in itself to have caused death. The wound
in the abdomen was frightful to look at, the bowels protruding. Short says it was the most horrible sight he ever
witnessed."

The Argus wrote that for a number of years McPartlan drove stage from Miles City to Junction, and "enjoyed
the friendship and good-will of everyone along the line,

possessing as he did, a woman's heart and a frontierman's courage."

U.S. Marshal W.H. Todd took McPartlan to Miles City to stand before a U.S. grand jury, the crime being committed on an Indian reservation. No witnesses appeared against McPartlan and he was discharged.

The River Press reported, "He has an excellent record there and his friends, of whom he seems to have many, feel satisfied that he never would have killed Moy except in self-defense."

He told the Press that the quarrel over his birthplace in Rhode Island was just Moy's excuse to pick a fight. "He had a quarrelsome disposition," McPartlan said.

In March 1929, the federal Board on Geographic Names made it official — to acknowledge the informal name given a mountain peak a few miles northwest of Lake McDonald where McPartlan died in August 1895. The peak, "Mt. McPartland," has the spelling generally used at the time of his death.

13

Elizabeth Collins Becomes the Mining Queen

October 25, November 1, 8, 2017

With the McPartlan boating accident behind her, Elizabeth Collins, Montana's cattle queen, started promoting the McDonald Creek mines.

Her missive published in the Sept. 20, 1895, Montanian and posted from Belton on the Great Northern Railway, began, "I left Great Falls on Aug. 27 with my cattle and although I struck a rather low market I got a good price. On my return I stopped at St. Paul, where I succeeded in interesting capitalists in the McDonald Creek mines.

"These parties are now shipping in supplies, tools, etc., to carry on development work during the winter on two locations, and if on sinking, the showing warrants it, they will build a concentrator, etc. Sixteen men have been put to work under Chas. Burton of Columbia Falls, as superintendent, to do the development work and to establish a winter camp at the leads. As soon as all the supplies for the mines, which are enroute from St. Paul, arrive here and are shipped up the lake, I will most likely return to Choteau.

"Parties of tourists are still arriving for Lake McDonald, but another month will likely see the close of the pleasure season for the present year."

A month later, the Montanian's headline was "The cattle queen now a mining queen. Something about the mines near McDonald Lake."

"Mrs. Nat Collins, having recently returned from Belton, has given some very interesting information about the McDonald Lake mining district. Mrs. Collins and her brother, Chan Smith, own half interest in five claims of quartz in that district, which is comparatively new.

"Eastern capitalists own the other half of these claims by virtue of having contracted to drive a shaft 200 feet deep. Mrs. Collins has been at the mines superintending the shipment of supplies for the winter and building camps. They are running a pack train of 15 horses and will, if the trail can be kept open, run pack horses from Belton to the mines all winter.

"The work is done in the name of the Montana Queen Mining Co. of which Mrs. Collins is vice president and resident manager. She has been so successful in getting capitalists interested in her properties that old miners have asked her to represent them in selling stock in claims they hold. Of course, she feels highly complimented by this turn of affairs.

"That Mrs. Collins is worthy of their confidence and esteem and will prove to be fully competent and a good rustler, admits of no doubt. She has been among miners all her life and knows how to treat them and is known also to be highly appreciative of any kindness shown her. By the way, she speaks very highly of our neighbor across the way — in Flathead County. She says that the reason the miners have sought her assistance in getting moneyed men interested with them is that she gets parties who are willing to work on an equality with them and don't demand a controlling interest before they do a lick of work or invest a dollar.

"Pearl Stokes and Marion Gleason are making winter camps about five miles from the above mentioned claims preparatory to working on a lead discovered this fall which shows on the surface about 100 feet of ore similar to the lead of the Montana Queen Co. Others are working on leads and the indications point to the opening of a large camp next spring.

"McDonald Lake is one of the finest summer resorts in the state and in all probability, many tourists will go there next summer for the double purpose of enjoying the fine scenery and salubrious climate and of taking advantage of opportunities of investment that exist during a good substantial mining boom."Mrs. Collins is now gathering cattle for shipment and will reduce her business here that she may devote more time to her mining interests. In this we see that we are apt to lose one of our best neighbors; a neighbor who proves a friend to the needy and a help in the time of trouble, the older residents of Teton will always remember her as such. Mrs. Collins will go to the Flathead valley and the good people of that country will win what we lose — a witty, sociable, intellectual lady."

During the following year, as Collins accompanied her eighth cattle shipment that fall, she was being labeled the "Copper Queen." The Collinses, with their daughter, Carrie, 16, spent the 1896-97 winter in Columbia Falls, the headquarters for the Collins's mining company.

In June 1897, Mrs. Collins told the Montanian that "the prospects of finding the hidden treasure is brighter than ever," about her mining claims at the head of Lake McDonald, but no major strike was ever reported.

Instead, Elizabeth set her sights on the Blackfeet Mineral Strip, the "ceded strip" as it was labeled when it was opened in April 1898. Its promoters quickly named it the "Montana Klondike."

The River Press reported, "At the appointed hour less than 100 boomers, including Mrs. Nat Collins, the Montana cattle queen, stood ready at the survey line near St. Mary's lake to enter the promised land. Four hours later stakes were being driven through 10 feet of slush and snow, marking the location of mineral and townsite claims.

"A careful estimate places the number of persons waiting at outside points, unable to reach the guard line on account of the swollen condition of the streams, at 500. No worse time for the opening of the strip could possibly have been selected. The prairie that composes the strip is naught but a mad torrent. Coulees, that during other seasons are dry, now are raging rivers, and several attempts to cross have been attended with narrow escapes from drowning. The bridge that crosses Black Tail creek has been washed away, shutting off the entrance of boomers from the south. At Summit a raging snowstorm is in progress, and as far as can be seen into the mountains from that point, severe weather prevails.

"So far as reported, the crowd have been orderly and no trouble is anticipated, although much talk of fraud and contest is indulged in."

The Teton Chronicle noted, "…among the misadventures reported from the Montana Klondike it is said that Mrs. Nat Collins, the Montana cattle queen, lost her horses while attempting to cross the Milk River, and herself had a narrow escape from death."

A week later, the River Press said, "Reports from the north are to the effect that Mrs. Nat Collins was 'the first man' to legally enter the ceded strip and stake out her claim. This was at St. Mary's lake, at noon on Friday last. The snow and slush was 10 feet deep, but 'that cut no figger,' the 'cattle queen' knows the country and when the snow goes off, it will be found that she has the richest claim on the strip — at least we hope so."

Not just content to have a mining claim, Mrs. Collins opened a restaurant and boarding house at St. Mary's lake, using her experience from her youth feeding the crews on long-distance freight wagon trains in Colorado.

The Anaconda Standard in September 1898 reported, "It is evident that [Mrs. Collins] has lost none of that adventurous spirit which led her to cross the plains about the middle of the century and cast her lot with the people of a new country.

"... Her friends will be glad to hear that she has thereby gained some mineral claims which she believes will prove compensatingly rich, and in this hope her friends will join her. Just at the present time she is back at her old home near Choteau.

"In a recent talk about the mineral strip, she said that there has been a great deal of lying done about the strip, and it naturally worked against the advance of the place. However, she has some assay returns, which look well, and her faith in the belt is not to be shaken, for she knows the place by heart. An assay made of rock taken on the Crocker [Cracker] lode, at the head of Boulder Creek, near Going to the Sun Mountain, shows the presence of copper, running from 55 percent to 75 percent. Mrs. Collins believes that this lode runs clear through the mountains to the Lake McDonald country, and George B. Grinnell, editor of Forest and Stream, who has been visiting that country recently on his annual hunting and fishing trip, took some of the rock home with him for further assay."

The Teton Chronicle in September 1898 reported on the doings of Choteau's cattle queen, turned "mining queen of the Crown of the Continent."

"Mrs. Collins looks hail and hearty and her looks do not misrepresent her. There are few women in Montana better known in the region of the Rocky Mountains and east as far as Chicago, than the wife of Nat Collins of Teton County. She is the whole team with the whiffletrees and neck yoke thrown in."

Other newspapers put a cynical spin on Mrs. Collins's exploits. The River Press on Oct. 19 republished a paragraph from the Helena Herald.

"The annual write-up of Mrs. Nat Collins of Teton County, nicknamed 'cattle queen' is on hand again this year. The Sunday Minneapolis Tribune devotes a couple of columns to a description of her career embellished with her portrait. This write-up contains the usual misstatements always made by eastern reporters about the Montana woman. She is put down as the owner of cattle 'on a thousand hills,' and all that nonsense. The old story about how she made the Great Northern allow her to ride in the caboose of the freight train carrying her cattle is also revamped. The guileless reporters always find a good Sunday article about this time of the year in Mrs. Collins's visits to the eastern stock yards."

Collins stayed east that winter to do a lecture tour she called, "Wanderings in the West." After she visited Plymouth, Indiana, in March 1899, the local newspaper wrote, "Mrs. Collins, in spite of her ranch duties and the cares of her great wealth, has time on her hands, and she recently visited the new mining region near St. Mary's Lake, Montana, and purchased a great tract of land, which she has just laid out into a town site and will found a town to be called Collins City. It is on the banks of the lake, rich in copper."

Alas, an old news search could not confirm a record for Collins City near St. Mary Lake, but Mrs. Collins did have a landscape feature to her credit. Although her mining venture on the west side did not amount to anything, there is a place called Cattle Queen Creek in Glacier National Park named for her.

Coincidentally, many people believe the unincorporated town of Collins in eastern Teton County is named for Elizabeth Collins. The book, "Place Names of Montana," however, says Teton County's "Collins" is named "in honor of Timothy E. Collins, a resident of Fort Benton, who was a stockholder and director of the Great Falls and Canada Railroad, a narrow gauge line built about 1890 from Great Falls to Lethbridge. The settlement was formerly called Brighton. A post office under Aeneas B. McDonald was in operation 1891-93; it reopened 1903-1961."

While the state mine inspector continued to say in January 1901 that the mineral claims up the St. Mary River and Swiftcurrent Creek on the ceded strip were going to amount to something, Mrs. Collins had already moved on. In October 1899, the Montanian reported that Nat and Elizabeth sold their ranch to Joe Baart for $500. Elizabeth headed east on a lecture tour while her husband, daughter Carrie and brother, Chandler, stayed in Choteau. Although never a healthy man, Nat began to dabble in politics under the Democratic party ticket.

In June 1900, the Dupuyer Acantha reported, "The great broad plains of the mountain state where once large bands of Mrs. Collins's cattle roamed, have now passed to other hands. Her stock has all been sold and for the first time in her life she has turned her back forever on the scenes that have surrounded her home for over a quarter of a century. In speaking with a friend last week, Mrs. Collins stated she would never again return to Montana. There her fortunes were made and lost and in new fields she will seek their recuperation. She is now in Seattle en route to Cape Nome, where she will open up a wild west show after the fashion of Col. Wm. Cody and also pay some attention to mining at which she is said to be an expert."

This newspaper report proved incomplete or inaccurate because the trip to Alaska was taken with the same enthusiasm that Collins attacked all her endeavors and she would not quit Choteau, in the end.

— 14 —
Elizabeth Collins,
The Later Years

November 15, 22, 29, 2017

With her husband and daughter nicely settled for the summer in the Swiftcurrent Creek valley west of St. Mary, Elizabeth Collins, 56, headed to the Alaskan gold fields in July 1900.

The Cattle Queen of Montana had become a Mining Queen as she prospected with partners in the Lake McDonald and St. Mary areas in what would become Glacier National Park. The gold proved elusive in northern Montana but the Yukon Klondike rush was in full swing.

In October the Dupuyer Acantha reported, "Mrs. Nat Collins, the cattle queen, arrived home from Cape Nome Saturday evening. She is very enthusiastic over her prospects there and intends to return in the spring. She brought a small quantity of the yellow dust of that place with her for exhibition. Capt. Evans, her mining partner, remains there this winter and the queen will rejoin him there in the spring."

The article said, "Mrs. Collins says there has been a vast amount of misrepresentation in regard to Nome by persons who went there thinking they could pick up a fortune on the sands, or secure employment at extravagant wages. She believes the country is rich, and that thousands of valuable claims will be worked within the next few years, but it requires hard work and some capital to do the work successfully. It is no place, she says, for a weak or lazy man.

"There was a good deal of sickness, but this was almost all caused by men neglecting to care for themselves and refusing to take necessary precautions or the time to prepare proper food. As Mrs. Collins expressed it, the great majority of the men live on tin cans. She says a great many women have gone to Nome, but she advises them against going unless they are accustomed to roughing it, are physically strong and can take enough money with them to bring them back in case they wish to return."

In December Collins wrote a column for the Montanian about her trip to Nome. She started with a description of the Seattle port, a favorite starting point for trips to Alaska. Her writing ability showed through.

"The departure of ships was delayed for days and weeks beyond the sailing dates advertised, on account of the ice remaining later that usual on Behring sea. The waterfront presented a lively appearance as day after day tens of thousands of spectators watched the loading and unloading of ships from all parts of the world.

"Commodities from every market in the world were offered for sale to thousands of ready customers. Fakirs of all imaginable tricks and novelties reached out for the almighty dollar, while sure thing games and confidence sharps reaped a rich harvest from the unsuspecting hayseeds from the New Hampshire hills and other rural districts.

"We counted 47 different kinds of gold-washing machines each of which was the only one that would really save the gold as could be readily proven by scientific demonstration. It is needless to say that hundreds of these machines were purchased and shipped north, only to be thrown away upon the beach as utterly worthless. One man was persuaded to buy a half cord of cordwood with which to stake out his prospective claims in the far north. His fellow passengers guyed him so much about it that he finally threw the wood into the sea.

"The ships began to sail away carrying from six to nine hundred passengers each and within a few days the population of Seattle was reduced by several thousands. The ships were invariably loaded down beyond their capacity, regardless of the comfort or pleasure of the passengers.

"The gold seekers as a rule hesitated at nothing, so impatient were they to get away to the Northern Eldorado. Instead of following around the coast, the ships, nearly all head straight for Dutch Harbor and travel a little north of west through the north Pacific Ocean for 2,100 miles.

"I went up on the steamer 'Newsboy,' laden with freight, horses, cattle and passengers. We encountered some bad weather and heavy seas, which caused some discomfort in the way of seasickness among the passengers, but withal we had an interesting and enjoyable trip and arrived at Dutch Harbor 12 days out from Seattle. Here we had an opportunity of going on shore while the ship took on coal and water," Collins said.

Collins, 56, came home from a prospecting trip to Nome, Alaska, in December 1900, and it seems she never returned.

She summed up her experience, "I have been in gold stampedes in New Mexico, Colorado and Montana, but anything I ever saw or experienced before sinks into oblivion compared with the Nome rush. In summing up the whole situation, however, I find that human nature is much the same, and all stampedes have about the same ratio of kickers, chronics and calamity howlers."

In March 1901 her husband Nat sold at auction, three-span work horses, three sets double harnesses, one 3.5 freight wagon (nearly new), one 3.25 freight wagon (nearly new), six pack saddles and equipment and tents and other camp articles.

Elizabeth went on a lecture tour again, staying in Montana, and although she continued to have mining interests, nothing of any consequence made the local news in that regard. Instead, her bookings on tour regularly made the papers and they described the special equipment she used for her talk, "Wanderings in the West," "ranging from the sublime grandeur of the Rockies to interesting sights witnessed by her in the land of the midnight sun."

"The illustrations were made and colored expressly for Mrs. Collins and are projected upon over 400 square feet of canvas by a powerful stereopticon, using calcium light," the Montanian wrote.

She earned the praise of the Businessmen's Association of Great Falls for her promotion of the state and her faithful descriptions of Montana given to people back east.

The next few years were spent in and around Choteau, and the biggest news for the Collins clan was the marriage of their daughter Carrie, 22, to Frank Salmond, 35, on Sept. 11, 1904. He was a prominent rancher and stockraiser on Willow Creek. They called the place, "Saypo," and Carrie's parents spent much time at the ranch during the next few years.

Elizabeth became active in the Society of Pioneers of Montana and spoke at its first business session in September 1907, while Nat spent his time over the years on the ranch and then, when that was sold, in Choteau. He was elected justice of the peace several times, including in 1902, and served as an alternate delegate in the Teton County Democratic Convention.

The couple celebrated their 33rd wedding anniversary in January 1906. The Choteau Acantha noted, "They are among the early settlers of Montana and Teton County, and are of that class of pioneers that have made Montana a great state, and though they have passed through the sunnier time of life and now stand where the autumn leaves are falling, they are receiving the sweetest of all life's gifts, the love and esteem of neighbors and friends."

Carrie gave birth to a girl, Tacie, in 1905, a son, John C., in 1907, and another girl, Rena, in 1913, but sorrow came to the family, too.

The Acantha reported on Dec. 29, 1910, "Mr. and Mrs. Nat Collins were made grandparents again and at twice the usual rate on Christmas Day when twin sons were born to their daughter, Mrs. Frank Salmond of Saypo. At last report, the mother and baby boys were doing nicely. It is safe to say that no man in the county received a more interesting Christmas present than did Frank Salmond."

The baby boys did not survive and Carrie was confined to her bed 25 miles west of Choteau when death came to her father, Nat, 78, who died on Jan 9. He had been sick for more than a week and died peacefully with his wife, Elizabeth, by his bedside.

Perhaps, the most ever written about him was penned in his Acantha obituary. It ended, "In his later years his physical strength failed; but he kept in their perfection, his mental faculties, so that conversation with him was at once interesting and pleasing. Uncle Nat will be held in affectionate remembrance as one of the kindest and most sympathetic of men, and all who knew him will be keenly conscious that a most gentle soul has passed from earth. The lessons of his long life were those of love and peace and truth. As citizen, neighbor, husband and father he lived without blame, and he died justified in the sight of men and of God."

After her husband died in January 1911, Elizabeth, 67, settled into the life of a soldier's widow, matron and grandmother.

Labeled a "cattle queen" and "mining queen" in the

newspapers, Collins was a frequent subject for features and the local columns. She was an important founding member of the local Old Timers Association and the Society of Montana Pioneers that had an annual conference each year.

She often visited her daughter Carrie and family at the Salmond ranch on Willow Creek, although the 25-mile wagon ride was challenging.

She sojourned at the health resort, Pipestone Springs, near Butte to recover her health that spring and she contended with diabetes mellitus, a chronic disease she would have for 20 years.

"Mrs. Collins says that she feels like another person since her stay at the springs," the Acantha reported in May.

She spent the summer of 1911 at Lake McDonald and traveled to California for the winter in December 1912. The Acantha reported, "The San Francisco Chronicle of a few days ago contains the picture of Mrs. Nat Collins together with the write-up which is reprinted below. Mrs. Collins is spending the winter in Los Angeles and recently spent a few days in San Francisco.

"'Mrs. Nat Collins of Choteau, Montana, famous throughout the country as the cattle queen of Montana and who was one of the first white women to enter that state, arrived in San Francisco yesterday for the first time in her picturesque and active life. Shortly after she arrived at the Manx Hotel, she took a trip over the city in a sightseeing motor car. After her return, she said:

"'I have spent a dollar many a time before and got a lot of enjoyment out of it, such as in buying an oyster stew, but I never got so much fun out of a dollar before as the one I have just parted with. Yes sire, seeing San Francisco was better than an oyster stew.'"

Alvin E. Dyer of the Dyer Printing Co. in Spokane, Washington, republished her 1894 book, "The Cattle Queen of

Montana," in August 1914. Access the 1894 work through The Digital Public Library of America. Another link takes one to the 1914 online copy in which Collins added a dozen pages about her Lake McDonald mining claims, her foray to Alaska and yet another variation of the death of Frank McPartland (McPartlan).

Readers should note that the 1954 Western film, "Cattle Queen of Montana," starring Ronald Reagan and Barbara Stanwyck, has nothing in common with the Collins saga, except maybe that both women owned cattle.

Collins's health began to fail. She was admitted to the Choteau hospital on several occasions in 1916, but recovered and visited friends in Coos Bay, Oregon, in May 1917. She spent the summer visiting friends near Seattle, Washington.

In January 1920, she fell down a flight of stairs but recovered. She visited her brother Chandler Smith in Preston, Idaho, in June and the Great Falls Daily Tribune wrote a long article about her life in September 1920, when she was the Society of Montana Pioneers' vice president during its 37th annual meeting, the last one she attended before she died.

Elizabeth Maud Collins suffered a cerebral hemorrhage four days before she died on May 28, 1921, 13 days after her 77th birthday. Her 20-year-long battle with diabetes was a contributing factor, her physician E.B. Maynard said.

Many obituaries recalled her long and eventful life. "She lived fully and found life in many ways worthwhile, but she was not unwilling, when her time came, to pass on to the next great frontier, beyond the Divide. ... The death of Mrs. Collins removes from the community a leading representative of the class of men and women who have helped to make the West what it is."

— 15 —

Running Rabbit's Rescue

January 4, 11, 2017

The well-regarded Blood Chief Running Rabbit made the newspapers as early as 1875 when he led his band of a dozen or more lodges from one location to the next, juggling for their survival while subject to the vagaries of the Canadian and U.S. governments.

Running Rabbit's whereabouts in Fort Macleod were noted in July 1881 when the River Press in Fort Benton stated, "The Running Rabbit, a Blood chief, has just returned from the American agency, and he tells the Bloods that they had better stay where they are, and that if they don't want to get whooped up they had better give the cowboys a wide berth; he says that the Americans have 'bloods' in their eyes."

In January 1882, the Benton Weekly Record noted under "Old Agency Items," the old name for Choteau, "Running Rabbit, chief of the North Bloods, is at the old agency, having come there from Macleod last week. He is 'out' with the Northern authorities and particularly with Major Crozier, who compelled him to pay duty on some sugar and a few blankets recently purchased of Hamilton and Hazlett of the Old Agency. He cannot understand how it is and thinks it robbery. When this misunderstanding occurred he pulled off his medal and chief's suit, which had been given him, and gave them back, saying that he was done with the Northern government forever. He then left with his family and came south of the line."

The chief contended with the short rations at the U.S. Indian agencies in 1884, food that had been promised by treaty as he settled on Two Medicine Creek on the Blackfeet Reservation. He survived the following encounter in August 1888, written up in Choteau's first newspaper, the Calumet.

"Running Rabbit and about 40 members of the Piegan tribe bought 125 head of horses from the Flatheads, but as they came through the Sun River area, someone reported them as being a horse-stealing party. Their camp was searched by Major Ronan, but not one stolen horse was found. Running Rabbit says that the whites can search his camp at any time. His people are not stealing any horses."

The first newspaper mention of Pennsylvania native Frank Pollinger was in March 1891 when, "High winds, accompanied by west snow, caused the Macleod-Lethbridge stage to be blown over. The stage driver, Frank Pollinger, and his eight passengers were unhurt. Pollinger was able to keep a firm grip on the reins so the horses stayed under control. He and the passengers went to the house of A.J. Whitney, where they spent the night, then continued to Lethbridge the next day."

By November 1896, Pollinger was south of the line, too, working a mail service contract that included stops on the reservation and parts south. And that is where the old Blood chief encountered the veteran stage driver.

The first report in the Nov. 27 Montanian read, "Last Monday a week ago Frank Pollinger left Blackfoot with the U.S. mail for Dupuyer. He left between 10 and 11 o'clock in the morning with a light buckboard and two horses. He should have been in Dupuyer that night. But he came not — not that night nor the next, nor since. He lies at the mission hospital with both feet and legs frozen half way to the knee and there they will have to be amputated. On

Wednesday Pollinger came to the house of Running Rabbit, about a mile from the mission, carrying his entire footwear, except one sock under his arm. One foot was naked and the frozen toes turned up as if broken by walking. On the other foot was the sock but that did not keep out the cold, though it kept the toes intact. His face and hands were but slightly frozen, strange to say.

"Running Rabbit took the frozen wanderer in and made him as comfortable as possible, but drawing out the frost with cold water and such other methods best known to the Indians. He also fed him and cheered the poor man up as best as he could."

The report went on to describe how bad the weather had been, "The snow was belly deep to a horse and still falling, obliterating every mark as fast as made and making traveling yet more difficult. The temperature, too, was severe, that Tuesday morning it was 30 below zero here at Choteau and could not have been much less on the reservation, 70 miles farther north."

Another version of the rescue, titled, "A Noble Red Man," appeared in a Great Falls newspaper two weeks later. The Montanian on Nov. 27, 1896, wrote a cringe-worthy story that had some new information in its last paragraph from George Smith: "We learn that Pollinger will not lose his feet, — not more than a toe or two at most; that when he unhitched his team Wednesday he was within 200 yards of Running Rabbit's house and in plain view of it, and that Running Rabbit went out at once and brought the bewildered man into the house and cared for him as before stated. George says that the Indian had a great time with Pollinger who seemed dazed and crazed with the cold, and that he would not submit to the former's treatment without a struggle. The poor fellow had to be held down all the while his feet were being bathed in ice water and rubbed vigorously until completely thawed out and the circulation restored. He is now under the mission doctor's care and will come out of his adventure nearly a whole man, thanks to Running Rabbit."

An updated version appeared in the Dec. 18 newspaper. John E. Stuart reported that he had never seen such a terrible blizzard in November. He said, "Frank Pollinger, the stage driver who was caught between Dupuyer and Kipp during the storm and badly frozen, is slowly improving. The newspapers were wrong in saying that he had been taken to the hospital at Blackfoot agency; he is still at the house of the Indian Running Rabbit on Two Medicine Creek, where he is receiving every care and attention. ...

"He is slowly recovering from the effects of his awful exposure to the elements, but will probably lose several toes. The Indian's family should be rewarded in some way for their kindness to the unfortunate man who would have perished in the storm had he not been rescued, and who would have probably lost his limbs and been crippled for life had it not been for intelligent and proper treatment after he was carried to the house."

The Dupuyer Acantha in April 1897 reported that Pollinger was "by no means recovered from that, to him, memorable storm. His right foot is well nigh useless yet and is swollen considerably, necessitating the use of a crutch, but it is improving steadily and will in a short time be as well as ever."

He got a job handling the lines on the north stage route the following September and opened a saloon in Cut Bank a year later. Alas, a year after that, in August 1899, he was charged with having sold whiskey to the Indians on the Blackfeet Reservation. Two months later he pleaded guilty in the U.S. Court at Butte. He was sentenced to 60 days in jail and a $100 fine. After that, he appeared in the 1910 U.S.

Census where at age 54, he was a farm laborer working for George Weed in Augusta.

Chief Running Rabbit, already an old man when he rescued Pollinger, died on July 30, 1903, in Browning at age 80. The River Press wrote, "Last winter he told his people here that he would depart for the happy hunting ground of the Indians at the beginning of the haying season. He was recognized by the Indians as their most famous chief, and he was the possessor of many medals of honor for services rendered, as he was at all times friendly to the whites."

And that may be one of the reasons a mountain in Glacier National Park is named after him. But that did not set well with well-known naturalist and park promoter Morton J. Elrod, who in December 1911, wrote in the Daily Missoulian that the U.S. Geological Survey's new edition of quadrangle maps of Glacier left something to be desired.

Elrod said, "The names that have been given and that have taken a place on the map are for the greater part such as should not find a place until other names are exhausted. ... I should like to see some authority that will abolish a long list of the frightful names now applied, even if there should be objection. ... Why should not Running Rabbit, Red Crow and all the other senseless names go?" Why, indeed. 〰

Cicero Bristol, The First Teton County Treasurer

September 28, and October 5, 12, 19, 26, 2016

Cicero L. Bristol had already spent a good deal of time in Montana by the time he was appointed Teton County's first treasurer in March 1893.

A New York native and Civil War veteran, Bristol, 54, and his family arrived in Beaverhead County sometime in early 1880, having come from Omaha, Nebraska, where he had been a pension agent.

He became a prospector at first, and then the proprietor of the Montana Railroad Hotel near Dillon. By February 1884, he was a trader running the post store at the Blackfeet Agency, near present-day Browning, for three years and then became a stockgrower and homesteader.

His wife, Mary, 35, died after a short illness in August 1880, leaving Cicero to care for his children, Lora, 12, and Leland, 4. He sent them back to Nebraska for a few years, then in 1885 they came to live on his homestead near Robare, north of Dupuyer, which along with Choteau were towns in Chouteau County back then. After a few years, Cicero sent them east for school.

So widower Bristol raised horses on his ranch, collected his war pension (he had been a sergeant in an Iowa infantry unit for three months and 10 days in 1863) and dabbled in politics. He was elected as the Burd Township officer in November 1888, and the Great Falls Leader newspaper effused, "C.L. Bristol of Choteau, an intelligent and staunch protectionist and descendant of an illustrious line of American ancestry, tracing far away back to the days of the immortal Cicero, is a very genial gentleman and perfectly amazed at the rapid progress of Great Falls."

He was the Robare delegate to the Republican Party State Convention in May 1892, and was appointed the voting registrar for the Robare district and later a judge for the November election.

His elevated stature made it easy for the Legislature to appoint him as the first treasurer of newly formed Teton County in March 1893. No matter that he had been arrested for grand larceny (theft) back in 1880 in Dillon. He had been ably defended and, "after a careful and thorough examination, he was discharged by Justice Estes. Although there have been some court cases here, this was the first of any interest," the Dillon newspaper wrote. He even served a stint as justice of the peace for Beaverhead County after that.

Besides, when appointed treasurer, he filed his official bond for $30,000 with W.S. Barrett, Geo. I. Smith, F. Truchot and E.E. Leech as sureties, an assurance that any malfeasance was covered.

And so Bristol's first order of business was to receive applications for licenses from "merchants, doctors, lawyers, saloonkeepers and others desiring to do business within the precincts of Teton County." His salary was $549.99 per quarter, the same as the clerk and recorder.

He has a grizzled appearance in the old photo in the 1988 Teton County history book, but he endeared himself in the community as a member of the local Literary Club and as a volunteer judge at the local spelling bee.

He told the Choteau newspaper, "People are now coming forward with their taxes in pretty good style despite the hard times." He even got a mention in the Anaconda Standard in December 1893. "Treasurer Bristol has collected county taxes very closely. Only about 130 names are on the delinquent list, and they are mostly small owners. Teton is the banner county in this respect," the newspaper wrote.

In March 1894, Bristol was elected vice chairman of the newly formed Teton County Republican Central Committee with Sam Mitchell, chairman.

The Republican primary in August was a bit different than it is now. The primary's purpose was to elect delegates who then held the convention. The county committee in August 1894 agreed that every citizen entitled to vote at the coming election and who would agree or promise to then vote the Republican ticket in November, was entitled to a vote in the primary. The polls were opened and kept open for an hour in 11 precincts, and 114 votes were cast. Bristol was one of the delegates elected and at the county convention at the end of August, the delegates elected Bristol as the Republican nominee for treasurer.

Teton County's first elected officials had been appointed to their seats, but in the fall of 1894, it was time for the voters to make choices. By September the ballot was set: Republican Bristol, Democrat George Steel and Populist Albion McDonald vied for the county treasurer's seat.

The Oct. 19 Montanian newspaper gave Bristol a glowing endorsement in the lead up to the November election.

"Among the candidates now before the people for endorsement of their past careers as public servants there is no man more worthy of an emphatic approval than C.L. Bristol, the Republican candidate for county treasurer.

"Mr. Bristol's work for the term soon to close has been of a character that stamps him as an official of strictest business integrity, and as a gentleman who has over striven to please as well as serve. For any Republican to be recreant

enough to party duty to vote against him is an act of disloy-
alty, which should be visited with swift political condemna-
tion and punishment in the future.

"The people of Teton County know a good man when
they find one, and hence we predict Mr. Bristol's election by
a splendid majority. Vote her straight boys, and you'll win,"
the Montanian wrote.

And Bristol did. He began a two-year term and found
the time in May 1895 to work on the Decoration Day committee on behalf of the GAR, (Grand Army of the Republic.)
He helped organize the July 4th celebration and served as a
judge in the school spelling bee. He presented an American
flag to the Choteau schoolchildren.

He got the sympathy of the community when the Dupuyer Acantha reported that his thoroughbred Morgan
stallion "Commodore" died at his ranch.

He endeared himself to the community when he began
riding a bicycle and got a group together to form a club in
June 1896. "The bicyclists headed by C.L. Bristol are taking
steps to rid the streets of Choteau of all bits of broken glass,
scraps of tin, nails, tacks, etc., liable to puncture their tires.
Two small boys were engaged for that purpose yesterday
and now one can ride with less danger of having a tire punc-
tured than formerly."

Soon it was time to nominate candidates for the November 1896 election. The Great Falls Weekly Tribune reported, "A nice question has arisen in Teton County politics
and the courts may yet be called upon to determine it. The
constitution of the state provides that no person shall hold
the office of county treasurer for more than two terms.

"When Teton County was created in the spring of 1893,
C.L. Bristol was appointed treasurer by the law that created the county. In the fall of 1894 he was reelected and is
now a candidate for renomination. The question is, can he,

if elected, serve; and legal advice in the matter has been already sought. He claims that he has not yet served two full terms, as contemplated by the constitution."

Bristol lost the argument when in September the attorney general said he was ineligible as he had indeed served two terms. The Republicans nominated Bert Hofer for county treasurer, but in November, he lost by nearly 100 votes to Hardy F. England, a fusionist. (A multiple party nomination; in this election, the Democrats and Populists were united.)

On Dec. 31, 1896, Dupuyer Acantha Editor C.E. Trescott wrote, "Hardy F. England, who was elected treasurer, does not take his office until next March. However, it is but fair in this write up to make mention of him. The treasurer is one of the most responsible officers in the county government and in Mr. England's hands, we believe the county funds will be as safe as they have been with Treasurer Bristol."

On Feb. 26, 1897, Montanian Editor S.M. Corson wrote, "On Monday next C.L. Bristol rounds out two consecutive terms in office as treasurer of Teton County. He will then turn the office over to Hardy F. England who succeeds him. May England's administration of the affairs of the office be as clean as has been Mr. Bristol's is all that can be desired of him."

And so it was with shock that county residents and Bristol's friends learned in July 1897 that Bristol had been arrested on a complaint charging him with embezzling county funds.

England took office on March 1, 1897, with the public's confidence that the county's finances had been in good hands.

The rented courthouse, known as the Burgy building in Choteau, burned down on March 20, but the county records were saved. Then State Examiner John G. Morony called on county offices on July 13 and 14 to look over the treasurer's records, normally a routine matter.

The Anaconda Standard broke the story first on July 29, and the Montanian in Choteau published an article the next day.

"Ex-County Treasurer C.L. Bristol of Teton County was arrested yesterday on a complaint charging him with embezzlement. He was arraigned before Judge D.F. Smith and in an answer pleaded not guilty and was released on a $1,000 bond. Bristol's term expired on March 1, last.

"For a month past the Board of County Commissioners of Teton County have been aware of a defalcation in the treasurer's office, but there was no way of ascertaining just what the amount might be. The manner in which the shortage was covered up, as contained in the information, is that on various dates certificates of redemption were issued to various parties for land that had been sold for taxes. Then the stub was torn from the redemption receipt book and no credit of the amount paid made on the treasurer's books.

"Through this method there is absolutely no check to tell how much money has been received by Treasurer Bristol and none will be, only as the redemption receipts are presented. It is said that already $435 has been discovered and the indications are that before the commission now at work on the deficit is through, it will run into the thousands. At the preliminary hearing before Judge Smith yesterday Bristol made no defense and was bound over to appear Oct. 4.

"The arrest caused the greatest amount of surprise and at first friends refused to believe it. Bristol has been a resident of Choteau for a number of years and has always born the highest reputation."

The story made it in all central Montana newspapers including the Great Falls Tribune that outlined the allegations in detail.

"A few days ago John G. Morony, state examiner, went to Choteau and proceeded to check up the books of the county officials. He found that Mr. Bristol's accounts were correct, according to the books, and was about to approve them. Then, it is alleged, application was made to the present treasurer for a certificate of redemption of certain land, which Mr. Bristol had sold for delinquent taxes. The applicant exhibited a receipt for the taxes, which, it is claimed, Mr. Bristol issued to the purchaser.

"It is alleged that no stub or other entry corresponding to the receipt could be found. Mr. Morony instituted a quiet investigation and secured several other receipts for delinquent taxes, purporting to have been issued by Mr. Bristol. It is alleged that no stub for any of these was found. Upon discovering the alleged discrepancy, Mr. Morony informed the county attorney and the result was the filing of the information.

"An official of Teton County who is in the city states that if Mr. Bristol is a defaulter in any sum whatever, the amount is over $2,000, as the sales for delinquent taxes on land which have not been redeemed amounted to between $2,000 and $3,000 during Mr. Bristol's incumbency of the treasurer's office.

"Mr. Bristol asserts that he will be able to prove his innocence and his friends claim that if there is any apparent shortage it is due to the loss of records."

County Attorney J.E. Erickson prosecuted the case, and J.G. Bair and James Sulgrove defended Bristol. The Montanian said, "The jury venire was nearly exhausted before a suitable jury was found. The evidence against him was so strong that there was no hope for his acquittal. He was sentenced to one year in the penitentiary."

But like the Phoenix, Bristol would rise again, and not

spend a single day in jail.

The community was in a state of shock at the verdict against the county's first treasurer, someone who served two terms in office, ending on March 1, 1897, with no complaints against his administration. State Examiner Morony found the irregularities that led to Bristol's arrest and conviction. He discovered that stubs of receipts for money paid to Bristol in the redemption of land sold for delinquent taxes were missing and that the money had not been accounted for. The apparent shortage was $435.15 (later reported as $531.20) at trial, but later records suggested that the shortage was at least $2,000.

Bristol, however, had the best defense attorneys in the county working on his behalf. After Judge D.F. Smith denied their motion for a new trial, attorneys Sulgrove and Bair filed a notice of appeal with the Montana Supreme Court. Smith was satisfied that Bristol would not attempt to escape and released him on a $5,000 bond, pending the appeal.

In the meantime, Bristol's bondsmen, who had covered his actions while he was treasurer, sent the county half the amount embezzled. In December the county commissioners ordered County Attorney Erickson (who would go on to be Montana's only three-term governor) to notify the bondsmen to make good on the balance of the shortage at once, or they would sue for its recovery.

So Bristol, 59, free while the appeal was ongoing, moved from his ranch north of Dupuyer and into Choteau, living off his Civil War pension. Amazingly, his name appeared on the delinquent tax list published in the newspaper in December for not having paid $49 in personal property taxes.

The *Montanian* noted, with no irony, that Bristol's son, Leland, graduated from Harvard six months later, on June 24, 1898, and in September Leland started a three-year course in law school.

Bristol continued to endear himself with his many friends throughout the summer. He took the school census when School District Clerk J.C. Gordon was ill. Local schoolgirls gathered and gave Bristol a surprise party in August 1898. "Mr. Bristol has, as he well deserves, a great many warm friends among the young as well as among the older people, and there is not a child in this city who has not in some way or other felt his kindness," the newspaper reported.

The attorneys' machinations over the summer delayed the appeal. They finally argued their case before a panel of Supreme Court justices during the last week of November, a year after Bristol was denied a new trial.

On Nov. 30, the justices reversed the district court's verdict on a technicality that must have had a few citizens smiling and shaking their heads.

The reversal was on the grounds that the term of court, at which Bristol was indicted by the grand jury and convicted, was irregular, in that it had been changed from the date originally named by the district judge.

"It appears that on Jan. 2, 1897, C.W. Pomeroy, then district judge, fixed a term of court for Teton County for the following July. Two days later D.F. Smith, his successor in office, changed the time to June. The term was held then and Bristol was indicted, tried and convicted. On appeal, his counsel raised the point that both grand and petit jurors were irregularly assembled, and that defendant should have another trial. The Supreme Court sustained the point and remanded the case, without considering the merits or demerits of his conviction," the Anaconda Standard reported on Dec. 1, 1898.

The Teton Chronicle labeled it a "very simple technicality," and throughout the winter, Bristol continued out on bond, pending a new trial.

The Dupuyer Acantha was the first newspaper to speculate that Bristol's retrial would not take place. In June 1899, Editor C.E. Trescott opined, "While no one seems to doubt the guilt of the accused, the opinion is freely expressed that he has been already sufficiently punished."

Bristol was now 60 years old. Finally in March 1900, Teton County Attorney Erickson filed a statement saying that a conviction was improbable if not impossible. Upon his motion, the case was dismissed without prejudice and the bondsmen released.

The news was so extraordinary that Erickson's court filing was published in full in the newspaper. He described the events of the case and stated that the evidence of Bristol's guilt was conclusive, but that circumstances had arisen since the trial, which forced a conclusion that further prosecution was inadvisable.

County Commissioners Clarence B. Perkins, M. Connelly and Wm. M. Foster requested that the case be dismissed. Their letter read in part, "We believe this to be the wish of almost all the large taxpayers and of the citizens generally of the county."

Erickson wrote, "While a request of this kind coming from the commissioners is perhaps unusual and while I am not absolutely bound by it, I do not feel at liberty to wholly disregard their wishes in matters of this kind involving the expenditures of the public funds."

He said many of the state's witnesses urged dismissal and the defendant's bondsmen had paid the full amount of the shortage. They too requested that the prosecution of the defendant be discontinued.

The bondsmen listed their arguments and charged, "We believe that the old gentleman can ill afford the expense of another trial of this case and that the only purpose which another trial would serve would be to harass him for those who in this county have political grievances against him."

That allegation did not set well with Erickson. He countered, "In their zeal in the defendant's behalf the bondsmen intimate that this prosecution has been conducted not so much because the defendant has committed a crime but rather for the satisfaction of those who have political grievances against him; this is an unjust reflection upon the officers of this court and has no foundation in fact. We have simply performed our sworn duty and prosecuted a man who openly and defiantly violated the plain provisions of the laws of the state of Montana, as fully appears from the records of the case."

In sum, Erickson said further prosecution of the old man was no longer warranted. "The defendant has doubtless felt keenly the force of retributive justice, no punishment can be more severe than the consciousness of having to pass the closing years of his life under a cloud; the prestige he once enjoyed is gone and he will probably never again occupy places of trust where he will be tempted to commit crimes," he wrote.

Case dismissed. Bristol worked at the Montanian for a time and together with its editor, S.M. Corson, competed with Trescott's Teton Chronicle. Then Trescott bought the Montanian and Bristol moved to his ranch on Birch Creek. Bristol's misdeeds, however, continued to haunt the courthouse. In April 1901, Bristol paid $172.41, the amount of another shortage that had been committed during Bristol's term.

With that, Editor Trescott concluded that sympathy was wasted on an embezzler. In June 1902, another small embezzlement came to light. "Where, oh, where will it end?" Trescott asked. He snidely said in the Aug. 15 edition, "Bristol left on yesterday morning's coach for Great Falls, no, not for good, gentle readers, but just for a day or two."

As for Erickson's suggestion that he never occupy another place of trust, in August 1905, Bristol was appointed postmaster at the dam site on St. Mary Lake, called Babb. Again Trescott snipped, "We believe the department could have done a d____ sight better in the selection of a stamp pounder, but the Rev. Hobab seems to have been lucky again," (a reference to Moses' father-in-law.)

The scandal ended. Bristol remained the Babb postmaster until he fell ill at age 77 and was admitted to the disabled soldiers home in Hot Springs, North Dakota, in the summer of 1914. He died in July 1917 and was buried in Wyuka Cemetery in Lincoln, Nebraska, his old stomping grounds, beside his son, Leland, 34, who had died in 1910.

— 17 —

Boom Towns

October 21, 28, and November 4, 2015

At least one writer in the Choteau newspapers in 1897 warned that no mineral wealth would be found in northern Teton County that could ever rival that of Butte or Last Chance Gulch in Helena.

"While I admit there is mineral to be found in the northern part of the 'strip' in the shape of quartz, it would take $50,000 to ascertain whether a paying mine could be produced. And as for the fabulous placer diggings that have been reported, it's all bosh," the writer said.

Promoters and speculators, however, induced the federal government to purchase the "ceded strip," for $1.5 million from the Blackfeet Tribe with an expectation of riches to come. The strip was opened for "mining purposes only."

Teton County, created in 1893, extended to the Canada border at that time, but Glacier National Park was not formed until 1910. When the ceded strip opened at noon on April 15, 1898, the "rush was immense," the Teton Chronicle said. Upwards of 1,000 people were already on the ground, but the snow was the deepest it had been in years.

The Chronicle complained on April 22 that not a worse day could have been picked. "About 60 men managed at the risk of their lives to get on the strip, and now that they are in, they wish they had not succeeded for they are standing around in slush up to their necks, without provisions and the majority of them will not be able to locate any ground for a week or more."

By May 27, the townsite of St. Mary had been located on the old homestead of Hank Norris, just outside the strip boundary and by July 15, post offices had been established there and at Swift Current, the next valley north.

Choteau businessman George Adlam and his partner sent favorable reports to the newspapers. "Already there are five saloons, three stores and two restaurants in the new town," Adlam said.

In July the Acantha reported, "James Harris came in from Swift Current Wednesday evening with a hat full of location papers for filing. In speaking of the 'strip' he says that but one of two things is certain concerning it: 'Either it is the greatest mineral district in the state, or it is a gigantic fraud, but what I have seen, and I have seen a great deal, leads me to believe the former to be the case.' Mr. Harris filed 20 location claims and returned the next morning to his bonanza."

The center of activity soon moved from St. Mary to Swift Current Creek where all the claims were.

In October 1898, a report cast a bit of gloom, but it wasn't enough to stop the prospecting. "The ceded strip a fake. Nothing but high altitude and mountain scenery. The vil... — beg pardon, the city of St. Mary is now a very quiet place indeed, with prospects of it becoming still quieter. The vast mines of wealth, which many looked forward to last spring, have proven to be a mockery, a delusion and a snare.

"The reports which several prospectors brought in of rich placer ground close by, have turned out to be fallacious, not to use a stronger term, and the specimen of $8,000 gold ore which was exhibited there is now said to have come from Arizona or some other warm place.

"As a matter of fact, it is impossible to get a 'color' in the neighborhood, and there is no mineral to be found within several miles. If there should ever be a town on the ceded strip, it will be at Swift Current. Some good looking copper has been found there and it is probably that in the future a camp will be established at that place, but the mines will require time and capital to work. It is decidedly not a poor man's country.

"When we left St. Mary, the population numbered about 26, with a fair prospect of further decrease. Adlam and Thompson were still running their saloon, but intended to close up shortly, Thompson returning to Choteau. Ed Mathews, who formerly ran a livery stable at Dupuyer, was fixing up a barn for his horses and will remain all winter, also Hanson, the store keeper; Stag Hound Bill; Two Dog Jack and his partner; Joe Harp and some others. The two last named are the men who bought the boathouse, and they intend to trap and hunt all winter. Gus Nordguist will stay with his saloon, and there will be a living for one saloon and a store. A number of cabins have never been finished and probably never will be.

"There will always be a village of some kind at St. Mary, but it is doubtful whether it will be much larger than the present town of Robare, unless some strike nearby. All present indications point to Swift Current. I have no desire to give the place a black eye, but the above is the truth about the present condition of the camp. Sic transit Gloria mundi. [Latin for 'Thus passes the glory of the world.'] G. Donnelly."

The St. Mary post office was discontinued in January 1900.

In December 1898, 500 pounds of dynamite was brought in to run a 100-foot tunnel at the Bull's Head copper claim. As the winter waned, a report came that Sam Dunbar confirmed the story of an alleged rich copper strike on Swift Current. "A few days ago a Swede miner and Billy Ellsworth arrived at Blackfoot from St. Mary's bringing with them some rich samples of ore, taken from a claim being developed by parties said to be in the employ of Marcus Daly and others. If the lead is anything like the samples submitted, the owners of the claim are said to have a very valuable property," the River Press in Fort Benton said.

The Acantha reported in April 1899, "Parties in from the ceded strip confirm the report that J.M. Harris has struck an exceptionally rich prospect at Swift Current. He has driven a tunnel in the mountain 50 feet and has encountered a body of ore into which he has entered 12 feet without finding the hanging wall. [Rock lying above the ore body.] The width of the ledge is therefore unknown. Assays show this ore to go 60 percent copper and $42 in gold. This is good news if true."

A report that summer said, "News comes from the Blackfoot reserve that A.M. Esler, the well known Helena mining man, who visited that region about a week ago, has bonded the Josephine and Bull's Head groups of mines, consisting in all of eight claims.

"The mines are in the Swift Current district and present a remarkable showing, the leads carrying both gold and copper. Some of the claims have shafts down from 50 to 70 feet and Mr. Esler believes that the extraordinary showing made at this depth justifies him in spending money looking for more.

"There are other claims also in the district which are being examined by mining men with a view to bond and purchase, and the prospect of a lively season in the ceded strip is very good indeed.

"Mr. Esler, who has bonded these mines, is well known throughout the United States as a mining promoter and the fact that he has taken an interest in the ceded strip shows that there is more mineral there than was thought last year," the Acantha said.

A second corporation, the Michigan & Montana Copper Mining & Smelting Co., was formed to mine the copper. It had 12 quartz claims to tap a ledge that was estimated at 25 to 40 feet wide. "Through this big ledge are found stringers of copper ore varying in width from six to 18 inches. On one of these claims they have a tunnel in about 70 feet, at the end of which there is a crosscut for 12 feet and in this crosscut several of these stringers of ore have been cut, the total being about five feet of ore. From three assays, which were made from 11 pounds of the ore from the crosscut, the average is $100 in gold, 16.5 ounces in silver and 48.5 percent copper," the papers said.

In September a new bit of gloom clouded the forecast but not yet concerning the mining claims. The ceded strip had been opened for mining purposes only, it having been designed as part of the government's "forest reserve," made to "preserve the timber, thus securing and preserving a larger water supply than there would be if there was no timber."

The Acantha reported, "What a fraud, this forest reserve so far as it applies to Swift Current country is concerned. Under its prohibitions no one can run a boarding house, or any place of business on the ceded strip. He may not keep a pig in his parlor or pen, have a milk cow to provide cream for his coffee nor keep a hen or two, to cackle at his door. It's got to go and the sooner the better."

Any uneasiness felt about the running of various enterprises, went away the following spring. A force of miners was busy drilling a tunnel for the Cracker mine in the side of a nearby mountain. The Swift Current post office moved to the new location with a new name, Altyn, established on J.M. Harris's flat, on the south side of the creek. Harris was the postmaster and Harris Hall was designated for a polling place in the coming November election.

The boom town of Altyn was born, but then Esler died of a heart attack at the Cracker mine. The miners' optimism dimmed but did not die with him.

"What effect his death will have on the mining interests of the Swift Current district it is hard to say. Those best informed say it will only delay matters for a brief time and that everything will move right along as before," the Acantha said.

These days, the ground is under water when Sherburne Reservoir fills to capacity, but the old town of Altyn, in the part of Teton County that once extended to the Canadian border was a newsworthy topic in its heyday between 1898 and 1906.

The talk was of gold, silver and copper at first, but the first two minerals were never found, an indication to never believe everything one reads in newspapers. The copper, however, was real.

The Swift Current mining district was situated on the ceded strip, in the northern part of Teton (now Glacier) County in the heart of the main range of the Rocky Mountains. The Acantha reported that the "scenery of that section is unsurpassed in beauty and grandeur anywhere on the continent. The mountains are high and broken up, many of them covered with snow the year round and there are innumerable glaciers. This strip of land, which was purchased from the Blackfoot Indians on April 15, 1898, by the government, was long ago known to be rich in minerals and this knowledge was the reason for the purchase. As soon as the strip was declared open for settlement to the whites, these claims were staked off and recorded and the work of developing them at once begun."

There was only copper, but worse for the miners, soon there was no Esler, the man with the money to extract the copper. After he died, the Michigan and Montana Mining and Smelting Co. bought the interests of the Esler Co. in its lease on the Cracker group of mines in 1901. It also bought the "concentrator" Esler had brought in at considerable expense, but that was never put in operation. With assurance that the mines would continue, the 300-plus residents of Altyn went on with the business of life.

Sam Somes in May put up a large hotel made from a carload of lumber and shingles from Kalispell. Walter Dalson put up a new building with a 12-foot ceiling and a glass front. Ed Lippincott got the contract for carrying the mail from Blackfoot to Altyn three times a week. Geo. A. Henderson set up a dentist office and the Falconer Bros. set up a butcher shop with a refrigerator.

"Altyn can boast of one of the best barber shops in the county. When you visit Altyn look it up. You will be well pleased," the Acantha said in July 1901.

The first child born in Altyn was a daughter to the wife of Frank Pike in July 1901. The first wedding occurred in August when Justice of the Peace Thomas Cowan married the couple, Sarah Spencer of Taylorville, Alberta, and Jesse Samples of the North Fork of Milk River. The Altyn string and brass band serenaded the couple and their guests.

The first load of ore from the Cracker mine left Altyn for Butte in August 1901. Manager W.P. Moore traveled with it so he could see what process was the best to treat it with before putting in machinery.

By September 1901, a telephone line was up between Altyn and the Cracker mine five miles away, and the community had a school under the direction of Hester Shattuck, and then Lillian Harris, the daughter of Altyn's founder, James M. Harris.

The reports of copper riches soon dwindled, although in October 1902 the Michigan and Montana Copper Co. had a crew of 15 working some 11 quartz claims.

Oil speculation followed the copper speculation with the formation of several oil companies in 1904, but one by one the wells were abandoned.

J.M. Harris, who had promoted Altyn for its copper, formed the Altyn City Oil Co., but in December 1905 his health began to fail, in part from a chronic injury he suffered three years earlier by falling into a mineshaft. In February 1906 he was adjudged insane and the district judge committed him to the asylum at Warm Springs. He died two months later.

The Altyn post office was abandoned in May 1906, although the school district continued for a time. A news account in 1912 noted, "Following the Swift Current [Creek] past Sherburne Lakes one reaches the deserted mining camp of Altyn. A dozen log buildings are all that is left of what once promised to be a bonanza mining camp."

A news article in 1923 said, "The Cracker Jack is abandoned, the road to the mill has gone to ruin, the mill is but a source of wonderment and questions for tourists, and the old town of Altyn has long since been dragged away, log by log, until now but a single cabin remains."

That is gone now. When hikers walk to the old townsite they see only the sunlight reflecting off the bits of broken glass and crockery scattered on the ground.

John Chouquette, Lawbreaker

John Chouquette, or "Choquette" as the news some-times spelled his surname, was the grandson of Charles Chouquette, the famous American Fur Co. voyageur, trap-per, interpreter and scout who was of great influence during Fort Benton's early days.

When Charles died in 1911 at age 89, the Forest and Stream magazine stated, "During his long life he was hon-est, sober, industrious, reliable, highly thought of by his neighbors and friends; equally esteemed by the bourgeois of the fur company for whom he might work, the chief of the Indian tribes among whom his work lay, or the superin-tendent of the Indian school on the reservation."

When John died in 1932, his accomplishments were of a different sort.

John was born in November 1888 (his birth year was also reported as 1886, 1887 and 1889) on the Blackfeet Reservation, the son of Charles's son, Henry Chouquette, whose mother was a Piegan Indian, and Henry's wife, Mary, whose maiden name was Gallineaux or Brockey, but who became the fourth wife of the warrior Chewing Black Bones on the reservation, after Henry died when John was a young boy.

John attended the Fort Shaw Indian Industrial School until the sixth grade. In July 1907 the Acantha reported that he was accused of stealing Douglas Boutelier's horse. At a preliminary hearing before Justice DeHaas in Choteau,

"Boutelier testified to missing the horse and finding him later in Choteau with brands altered, and appearance otherwise changed. Peter Grande, an Indian from near Browning, testified as to a conversation between himself and Chouquette in which the latter stated that he had taken up the horse near Choteau. The defense introduced no evidence," the Acantha reported, and John was put in the Teton County jail in Choteau.

On July 27 Chouquette and fellow prisoner John Wilson "made their escape from the county jail by digging out through the wall. They used a piece of water pipe about 3/4-inch in diameter, which had been used in the jail as a poker. With this they broke the concrete and removed stones enough to permit of their passing through. The wall is built of boulders, and the concrete had become soft.

"Wilson, who recently finished a term at Deer Lodge for horse stealing, was awaiting trial on another similar charge, and is also wanted by the Canadian authorities. Chouquette was recently bound over to the district court charged with stealing Douglas Boutelier's horse," the Acantha reported.

Chouquette was captured on Aug. 1, eight miles west of Dupuyer by Deputy Sheriff Harry Kunkel, acting upon advices from Undersheriff Ganong.

"Chouquette had supposedly been staying among the [mixed blood Indians] in the canyons along the mountains. He was retaken while on his way to the reservation and lodged in the Dupuyer jail, whence he was brought to Choteau Friday evening," the Acantha reported. He was arraigned in the district court and charged with grand larceny and later that day he pled guilty and was sentenced to 18 months in the state penitentiary.

He entered the Montana State Prison on Aug. 8, 1907, and was discharged on Dec. 7, 1908.

A year later on Dec. 2, the Acantha reported, "For the

second time within the past year, the town of Collins has been the scene of a daring hold-up. Some months ago the saloon of Ben Feist was the victim, the lone robber who did the job getting away with about a hundred dollars. Last Monday evening, about eight o'clock, five masked men, six, according to some reports, got away with another smooth job in the town.

"Three of them entered the store of the Boorman Mercantile Co., a new establishment at Collins, leaving two on guard outside. They ordered the proprietors and four customers in the store to throw up their hands. The command was at first taken as a joke, but this notion was quickly dispelled when the robbers flourished a number of dangerous looking guns. The customers were relieved of their cash on hand, except one man who managed to conceal the greater part of his funds. Then the proprietor of the store was forced to hand over the contents of the till and a bundle of bills, which the first had just received, amounting to $800."

The Acantha recapped the robbery in Collins in December 1909, noting that the robbers appeared to have knowledge of the till contents.

"The company lost in all about $875 in cash besides canned goods, knives and other articles which were carried away in a sack. A train crew who happened to be in town were relieved of about $90. After leaving the store, the bandits ran westward toward the Teton, and nothing more was seen of them.

"Upon leaving the store they threatened to shoot any man who ventured out, the leader stating that they were going to the Feist saloon to continue their work. This, however, seems to have been a bluff, as the saloon was not disturbed," the Acantha reported.

"Among those who were in the store at the time of robbery was John Brolsma, of Farmington, who was at Collins for a load of freight. Ted Hawley, of Choteau, was another victim, and J.E. Cashman, the Bynum sheepman, was also in the town, though it is not known that he was held up. Wallace Coburn, one of the best rifle shots in the state, was returning from Sun River canyon with a shipment of game, and had his rifle and ammunition with him, but did not know of the trouble until it was all over with," the Dec. 2 Acantha stated.

In a shorter article in the same edition, readers learned that the robbers had been captured. Four men were in custody and one was drowned in the Missouri River near the mouth of Belt Creek, east of Great Falls. "The robbers were captured at Great Falls, having turned back to cross the Missouri at the bridge. Most of the property taken was recovered. The captives will be in Collins tomorrow," the Acantha reported.

The suspects were arraigned in Choteau on a charge of having robbed a sheep camp belonging to August Kropp, and a few days later they were arraigned on bench warrants for the robbery and all pleaded not guilty. Bail in each case was fixed at $5,000. The suspects gave their names as Frank Collins, George Wilson, Clark or Jack Allen, alias Jimmy Clark; and John Chouquette (also spelled as Choquette). "Slim" Kelly was the drowned suspect.

Wilson was white, and the others were part Indian. On Dec. 13, 1909, Chouquette changed his plea and in court, pleaded guilty to the charge of robbery.

"The sentence was put over to the afternoon at two o'clock, when Judge Ewing pronounced it as 20 years at hard labor in the state prison. The fact that Chouquette had already served a term made his sentence more severe than it otherwise might have been. It is said that he was considerably affected by the sentence," the Acantha reported.

Chouquette's prison record lists his age as 25, occupation

cowboy, and noted that he would get out of prison with good time earned on March 15, 1921.

The River Press in Fort Benton reported that Chouquette was the first of the Collins holdup men to be arrested and it was from him that County Attorney O.D. Gray obtained a full confession that was going to be used in the prosecution of the three other prisoners.

"Chouquette entered a plea of guilty to the charge of robbery probably with the belief that his act would result in his obtaining a light sentence, but as it is known that he has been involved in a number of cases of horse stealing, and has once served a term in prison for such an offense, his record was probably taken into consideration by Judge Ewing in passing sentence.

"In his story to the authorities Chouquette insisted that he had been forced to join the bunch which pulled off the Collins affair and although he wanted to get away from them he was afraid to make a break for fear that the others would take his life. He told a complete story of the affair from beginning to end and placed much light upon the movements of the gang as well as upon other gangs of horsethieves who have been working in the northern part of the state for a number of years."

The other holdup men pleaded guilty in March 1910 and Judge Ewing passed sentence in the Teton County Courthouse. Wilson, 25, and Allen, alias James Clark, 28, were each given 20 years. Frank Collins, 18, the youngest man in the bunch, was given 10 years, his youth gaining for him some consideration.

The River Press in Fort Benton reported that Collins said he had been led into the crime by "Slim" Kelly, the fifth member of the party, who drowned.

Chouquette's famous grandfather, Charles, died in 1911 on the Blackfeet Reservation, while John remained in prison where he took up playing in the prison band. The Butte Daily Post noted in May 1917, "The Sunday afternoon concerts by the Montana State Prison band are ever growing more popular, and residents not only of this city, but also those of Butte and Anaconda have been numbered among the recent audiences." John Chouquette performed a baritone solo in those concerts.

In the meantime, prison inmates had to fill out draft cards. John's card says he was born on Nov. 15, 1888, meaning that he had just turned 21 when he was sent up for the robbery.

He must have been a model prisoner, or perhaps the U.S. military authorities were short of men to serve, because the State Board of Pardons commuted his sentence shortly after the Board's official hearing on Jan. 3, 1918.

At some point after that, Chouquette entered the Army. He served at least six months as a private in the 27th Spruce Squadron. It was one of many small construction and logging units working in the spruce forests of the Pacific Northwest providing lumber to make warplanes. He would have been mustered out no later than February 1919 at Vancouver Barracks.

One month later, Chouquette, 30, and Margaret Jackson, 22, both Indians and residents of Glacier Park, were married before a justice of the peace in Cascade County. The Great Falls Tribune stated, "The groom was recently discharged from the service of the military, his marriage to Miss Jackson occurring upon his return from Camp Lewis."

John worked as a laborer but he could not avoid trouble. He was indicted for bootlegging by a federal grand jury in December 1919, but nothing came of that. In September 1921, he was arrested for allegedly being in a drunken condition on the Blackfeet Indian Reservation with whiskey in his possession, but that charge was dismissed upon the grounds that insufficient evidence to convict was obtainable.

Chouquette settled into family life. The couple had a daughter, Lois, in 1923, and John got a job as a musician teaching in Browning schools. Then an altercation occurred on Nov. 27, 1926, with Frank Edwards, 22, at a party at Olive Racine's place in the vicinity of Badger Creek.

Chouquette was charged with manslaughter. The Helena Independent Record reported "considerable whiskey" was consumed and Chouquette admitted on the stand that he had been drinking.

"None of the witnesses of the scuffle, in which Edwards was fatally wounded, testified that they saw the actual stabbing. The lights in the Racine home were dim, it was claimed. John Russell, the state's principal witness, however, testified that he saw a knife in Chouquette's possession after the incident. Edwards and Chouquette became embroiled in an argument, which led to a physical encounter. Soon after they grappled, it was testified, Edwards dropped to the floor and yelled, 'I'm shot!' Later he moaned, 'I'm stabbed!'"

Edwards was taken to the Cut Bank hospital, where he died on Dec. 2. A jury convicted Chouquette, 38, of manslaughter and on Jan. 17, 1927, Glacier County District Judge John Green of Choteau sentenced him to a term of five to 10 years.

It's not known whether there was a prison band to join this time. John died on April 2, 1932, and thanks to his six-month stint in the Army, he has a fine marble tombstone on his grave near his grandfather's unmarked one in Holy Family Mission Cemetery near Browning.

19

Forest Ranger Lorenzo Jefferson

Lorenzo Jefferson grew up with the Lewis and Clark Forest Reserve for his backyard, and it was an added benefit that the federal government's forests were where the best jobs were.

Choteau was the forest headquarters, and the local newspapers kept readers informed of the forest news as early as 1900 when the Lewis and Clark forest was selected for timber harvest. "It is chiefly in a broken and little-known region, but has valuable forests and the timber is locally in demand," Washington bureaucrats noted.

Jefferson, who was nicknamed "Duff," was born on a Belleview ranch in 1892. He attended school in Choteau, and in 1909 the family moved to a new home in Fairfield.

Jefferson, 16, was too young to apply for the first forest ranger examination held in September 1909 under the auspices of the Civil Service Commission.

Applicants had to be between the ages of 21 and 41, be residents of the state, and had to have a strong physique and be capable of performing hard manual work.

"Experience is the most essential qualification, although ability to make simple maps and write intelligent reports upon ordinary forest business is required. Exam covers knowledge and experience required in conducting national forest work. Written tests include land surveying, estimating and scaling timber, logging, land laws, mining and livestock business," the Acantha said.

"The field tests cover the same subjects as far as practicable, together with packing and other work necessary in the administration of the national forests. Initial salary paid to first rangers is $75 per month.

"Where saddle and packhorses are necessary in the performance of their duty, rangers are required to own and maintain them. The Forest Service furnishes no personal or horse equipment.

"Under direction of forest supervisors, duties include patrol to prevent fire and trespass, estimating, surveying and marking timber, and the supervision of sales. They issue minor permits for the use of national forest lands, build cabins and trails, oversee grazing business, investigate claims and report upon arrest for violation of national forest laws and regulations.

"It is the policy of the forest service to fill vacancies in the higher positions by the promotion of rangers and the opportunity for the rapid advancement of competent men is an excellent one," the forest service stated.

Forest Supervisor W.H. Daugs supervised the test for the first eight applicants.

The Oct. 28, 1909, Acantha reported, "The first test was held Tuesday at the fairgrounds, and was interesting in an unusual degree. The applicants were required to bridle and saddle a horse, to pack another with tent, bedding, tools, etc., and ride at a gallop. Other requirements were reading a compass, estimating distances by pacing them, arriving at approximate areas by pacing the dimensions and identifying four of the principal forest trees from branches bearing the cone as well as the needles.

"The first test, especially the packing, was decidedly interesting to the spectator not familiar with such work. The applicants went at it as if they knew their business, and Supervisor Daugs stood by, watch in hand, taking the time consumed and making notes on the work of the applicants. Considerable amusement was aroused when the packhorse bucked with the load which Prince Townsend, the first applicant, strapped on."

Jefferson had much to learn before he could take the ranger exam himself, but he had an edge — his older brother, Frank, passed the ranger exam in October 1910. Lorenzo took a job driving a delivery wagon for the Choteau Mercantile Co., biding his time, and soon he got a break, and was hired as a "forest guard" for the summer in 1912. The Acantha reporting on the July 4, 1911, celebration in Choteau, said that Lorenzo, riding a horse belonging to John Smith, came in second in the cowboys' saddle horse race.

By 1912, six rangers worked on the Lewis and Clark Forest that was segmented into the Lubec, Teton, Sun River, Willow Creek and Dearborn districts, and Scott Leavitt had replaced Daugs who transferred to a forest in Idaho.

Finally, Lorenzo was old enough and he took and passed the ranger exam in October 1913. In January 1914 he attended a 12-week course in forestry at the University of Montana in Missoula, and by April the Acantha reported he was settling in to his first assignment based out of the Ear Mountain Ranger Station.

While not very glamorous, the job was part and parcel of his duties. "Duff Jefferson spent the first part of this week repairing the Forest Service and the North Teton telephone companies' lines between Choteau and the Teton canyon," the Acantha said.

As the Acantha reported after that, his career included transfers to other stations along the Rocky Mountain Front, the same as his older brother, Frank, who had passed the ranger exam three years earlier.

"E.A. Woods, forest ranger, is moving from the North Dupuyer station to the Beaver Creek station on Sun River.

Duff Jefferson is to have charge of the Dupuyer Creek district and Stanley C. Sanderson, the Teton district," came a report in May 1914.

That summer held more news, with all hands on deck: "One of the worst forest fires in the history of the Lewis and Clark National Forest" was reported on Aug. 13, on the ridge between Wrong Creek and Sun River opposite the mouth of Seven-up Creek.

"Within 24 hours approximately 200 men and 70 pack horses were on the fire line," the Acantha reported on Aug. 19, 1914.

Having started on a Thursday, the fire was under "good" control by Sunday night, with rain and snow falling the next day.

In the aftermath, "Duff Jefferson is suffering from a badly injured hand, the result of being struck by the forefoot of a vicious pack horse," the Acantha reported.

Jefferson settled at the Pike station in the Lubec district (the northern edge of the Lewis and Clark Forest) in August 1915. In September he and assistant Sylver White finished a grazing reconnaissance on their district and reported that instead of 10,000 sheep, 18,000 could be run there during the next year.

In October Jefferson married Charlotte McKay in Great Falls. She had been a stenographer in the local forestry office. The couple took up residence in the Lubec Ranger Station. Their union lasted until his death, and it included four children.

In February 1917, Jefferson was down from the Willow Creek station near Augusta issuing permits to ranchers who desired to enter their stock on the forest reserve that year. In October 1918, he was over from Augusta to attend the James Johnston funeral in Choteau. The forest ranger from Dupuyer had taken the ranger exam with Jefferson, but he died of pneumonia, following the Spanish influenza, while being stationed at Ear Mountain.

Having worked every location along the Rocky Mountain Front, Jefferson got a promotion in November 1919 when he was appointed ranger in charge of the Highwood division of the Jefferson National Forest, according to an announcement made by W.B. Willey, supervisor.

In the meantime, Jefferson's older brother, Frank's career in the Forest Service was evolving. When he died in February 1953 at age 63 he held the post of chief fire control officer of the U.S. Forest Service, Region 5, with headquarters in San Francisco.

Duff Jefferson's comments made the Great Falls newspaper every so often and in March 1920 it reported, "Between 30 and 40 head of cattle have been destroyed by the wolves in the Highwoods this winter, according to L.F. Jefferson.

"D.W. Griffith of the biological survey has been assigned to the Highwoods to eradicate these animals and during the past few weeks has trapped six wolves."

In July 1920, Jefferson was transferred again, this time to the Missoula Forest office at Phillipsburg, and in December 1922, he was the district ranger in the Lolo Forest. In July 1925, he was the deputy supervisor of the Beartooth National Forest, then the assistant supervisor at the Pend Oreille National Forest in Sandpoint, Idaho, and finally, the supervisor of the Clearwater National Forest in Orofino, Idaho, in the early 1940s. The Teton County native retired to California and died in December 1955 at age 70.

And he never forgot his stint as a forest guard. In an essay published in a Forest Service Bulletin in January 1939, he successfully pitched a proposition to place guards and many other seasonal employees on the Civil Service rolls.

"There are men in this territory who have grown old,

decrepit, and nearly blind on the 'guard' job, and who have been dropped or are ready to be displaced by younger men. It is a distasteful task to inform an old man, whose loyalty, interest, and energy have been devoted to Forest Service work for years, that further work is not available for him."

20

Mountain Mysteries

The rugged mountains west of Choteau had their share of mysterious incidents published in the early newspapers.

On Dec. 2, 1898, the Browning writer for the Teton Chronicle in Choteau reported that a few years ago Blackfeet Indian Agent Major George Steel lost 42 head of cattle. The stock had been in the habit of ranging together near his home, but suddenly they disappeared.

They were at last given up as lost at the time, but then during the past summer, the story went, an old prospector came upon the skeletons of 42 head of cattle far back in the mountains and up on a ridge.

The correspondent said the bones matched in sizes to the ages of the Major's lost stock and without a doubt they had worked back into the range where they remained until the snow got too deep for them to get out and so died from exposure and starvation.

On Jan. 27, 1910, the news reported that George Sturgeon, 16, left home in Conrad on the previous Saturday after saying he was going to the family ranch on Sheep Creek near Dupuyer. Arriving at the ranch, he took a saddle horse, some provisions and a pair of blankets and announced his intention of going into the mountains, even though the ranch hands tried to dissuade him.

He next appeared at Griff Jones's ranch at the mouth of Birch Creek Canyon, where he stayed overnight. Jones advised him not to go into the mountains and the boy turned back.

However, he turned his horse loose a short distance below the Jones place and started into the mountains on foot. His horse returned to the ranch the following day saddled and bridled, and aroused the alarm of the people there.

Word was at once sent to Conrad and Mr. and Mrs. Sturgeon shortly thereafter arrived at the ranch. They learned that George had said that he was going in to Chick Grimsley's hunting camp, which was some 60 miles in the mountains at the head of Big River.

Feeling easier about him, the Sturgeons turned back, but sent a man on to Grimsley's camp to make sure no harm had befallen the boy. When the man reached the camp he found that the young man had not been there, and so he began a search.

Some distance east of Grimsley's camp, he found the boy's coat and gun. Continuing the search, he found George's body on Sunday morning there in Birch Creek Canyon, somewhere near the summit. The mystery was never solved as to why George was dead set on getting to the camp in one day.

Two years later, in August 1912, the Choteau Acantha reported that the skeleton of a man who probably met his death six months before, or even longer, was discovered at the foot of a precipice in a coulee in the breaks of Birch Creek north of Valier.

A man, who was fishing in the stream, noticed a boy holding a skull he had found. The fisherman followed up the coulee and passing through some brush at a distance of 200 yards discovered the rest of the skeleton. The flesh was gone entirely from the bones, and only a few pieces of clothing were left. The ribs were broken along one side, also the bones of one ankle.

At first it was thought that the remains were those of

a former manager of the Empire Lumber Co. at Valier, who disappeared some time back, leaving word that he intended to take his life. His wife, however, was positive that the remains were not those of her husband. No one else was known to have disappeared from the Valier country.

County Coroner Chas. Connor decided that no inquest was required. The remains were taken to Conrad for burial, closing the matter as an unsolved mystery.

And then there's the case in December 1965 of Clara, age about 4,000 years old, the Acantha reported.

Clara was the name given to the skeleton of a bison discovered by Jim Brewster, packer for the U.S. Forest Service, just east of Cleary (Clary) Coulee. The backbone, head, lower jaw, and teeth were all that remained.

Forest Ranger Vergil Lindsey said two archeologists from the University of Montana took the skeleton to Missoula for study and display. They dug out Clara on the way back from Helena, where they dug up the jaw of a rhinoceros, which had considerable seniority over the bison.

21

Cortlandt W. Dawe,
Addict and Accused Killer

November 16, 23, 30, December 7, 14, 2016

The Daily Missoulian and the Great Falls Tribune were the first to break the news of a murder in Valier that had happened on Nov. 16, 1913.

Great Falls — Nov. 17. "Near Valier, about 80 miles north of here, in the center of a newly irrigated section, Charles Clifford, known as 'Chaparral Charley,' a settler, was shot down on the road on his way home from Valier. Dr. Dawe, a neighbor, who informed the authorities of finding the body, was arrested following an investigation by a deputy sheriff, and is in jail. So far no motive is known for the shooting, and except that Dawe had been drinking, there appears to be little evidence against him.

"Clifford was an inoffensive man about 60 years of age, and Dawe is about 30. The latter previously was the contract doctor for the irrigation work, but had not been in the employ of the contractors lately."

The Choteau Acantha and Choteau Montanan newspapers had the story on Nov. 19, 1913, reprinting a longer Tribune account, two days after the coroner's inquest.

"Late this evening Deputy Sheriff Peter Moran took Dr. Dawe, a homesteader living about 10 miles north of this place into custody, following an inquiry lasting all day into the murder last evening of Chas. Clifford, another homesteader, and more commonly known as 'Chaparral Charley.'

The coroner's jury which sat at the inquest into the death of Clifford returned a verdict in the formal language this afternoon, announcing that Clifford came to his death as the result of a gunshot wound from a weapon held in the hand of a person unknown to them.

"This, however, was but a formal portion of the proceeding, and after vigorous work all day, Deputy Moran decided to take Dr. Dawe into custody, and the prisoner was taken to Conrad tonight by the deputy and locked up there.

"So far, as has yet been discovered, there are no witnesses to the killing of Chaparral Charley, but the officers and those who have been investigating the case believe it was an insane impulse of quick origin.

"Even with the arrest of Dawe, there is missing any motive unless it be found in the possibility that the act was done as the result of too much dissipation at the saloon while he was at Valier yesterday, though even that has not been established as yet."

A six-man jury heard the testimony at the inquest on Nov. 17 at the Hotel Valier of homesteader Dr. Cortlandt W. Dawe, Valier physician Dr. Leland Botsford, homesteaders William T. Bell, Robert Emery and Matt Westub; U.S. Marshal Ralph Broadhead, Valier attorney J.A. Phillips and Valier carpenter Albert Freek.

Dawe testified at that inquest that he found the mortally wounded Clifford on the road outside Clifford's fenceline and carried him to the house and tried to give him aid. He went over to his own house about 80 rods away to get Bell, and afterward Bell went to get Emery and a decision was made to get a doctor and the sheriff.

Bell testified that Dawe came to him at Dawe's house to say that Clifford was hurt and when they arrived, Clifford was on the house floor. Dawe told him he found Clifford on the road and carried him in. He said he never heard a shot.

Clifford died from a gunshot wound to the neck.

Dawe's testimony sounded plausible, but on Nov. 29, Teton County Attorney D.W. Doyle filed an "information" that Dawe had committed murder on Nov. 16. He "did willfully, unlawfully and feloniously and with premeditated malice aforethought shoot and kill one Charles Clifford with a loaded pistol and did thereby kill and murder him."

Doyle's version was that Dawe came to Valier from his homestead about 11 miles north of town and while there became somewhat intoxicated and quarrelsome. He was arrested and confined in jail for three or four hours and about 5 p.m. started for home on horseback.

At about 6 p.m. he arrived at home and while Bell was tying up the horse, Bell witnessed Dawe and Dawe's mother struggling over something, which was a gun and that the younger Dawe ran over to Clifford's house. Doyle's story continued that Bell heard a shot and that Dawe was on a tear intending to kill Emery, too.

What happened to bring about two versions is lost to history, but Dawe was arrested and pled not guilty. He was remanded to the custody of the sheriff without bail on Dec. 3.

Dawe, 33, testified at the inquest that he came upon his mortally-wounded neighbor on his ride home from town. William Bell, who was staying at Dawe's ranch, said he did not hear a shot. Dawe arrived home and told Bell to get neighbor Robert Emery. Emery picked up Dr. Botsford and when they arrived at Clifford's place, the man was dead. Botsford thought he was shot in the neck by a high-powered rifle no closer than six feet away because there were no powder marks.

Emery testified that Clifford was afraid for his life. "Several times he was afraid somebody was after him and I asked why, but he didn't seem to tell me much," Emery said.

"Trouble over water?" the coroner asked.

"This place that Mr. Stettler has [Clifford was the tenant] is practically the only water we have and all of us get water there and during the hot weather the well did not produce enough to supply all the people and quite a few of us were asked not to take water at night when Charley wanted the water for his horses," Emery said.

Matt Westub's testimony at the inquest, however, pointed to Dawe. He said his house was on the other side of Clifford's from Dawe's and Dawe came up riding "pretty fast."

"Would you say he was sober?" the coroner asked.

"Well, I don't know. He knew me from far away and then I went to him and said to him that he was riding too hard and his horse was all wet and he started off and said, 'I give him Hell now,' and drove away fast."

"He acted like he had liquor?"

"Well, I don't know," Westub said.

U.S. Marshal Ralph Broadhead's testimony included an encounter with Dawe on the afternoon before the shooting and a discussion of Dawe's gun.

"Did you see Dawe?"

"Yes. Yesterday, the doctor was drunk and I was called to take care of him and I took him from the hotel to the fire house where I stay and kept him there until sometime between 4 p.m. and 5 p.m. Then I rode with him out of town to the other side of D.F. Mains' [place] and I searched him before he left town and Al Freek searched his overcoat and took some booze out of his pocket and I searched his small coat and his pants."

"Did he have a gun?"

"No," Broadhead said.

He later retrieved the 32-caliber gun at Dawe's home and said he was sure the gun had not been fired. "He did not have a gun when he left town," Broadhead said.

"What is his [Dawe's] nature when he is full [of liquor]? He wants to fight?" the coroner asked.

"Yes, sir," Broadhead said.

Valier attorney J.A. Phillips, a self-proclaimed gun expert, examined the gun and told the coroner's jury it had not been fired.

There's a thick document in the Teton County Courthouse that reveals the complex pathos and mystery behind this tragic incident.

Three physicians, Dr. Nelson Young, Dr. R. Harvey Cook and Dr. George Rusk Love, and U.S. Army Medical Officer Basil Dutcher testified in depositions that Dawe suffered in the past from chronic alcoholism and a morphine and cocaine addiction that would have rendered him mentally irresponsible and temporarily insane, assuming Dawe fired the shot.

But we're getting ahead of ourselves. The Dawe case was set for trial on March 17, 1914. The attorneys selected a jury of 12 men and H.W. Yeager would be elected foreman during the deliberation.

"This case will probably last the balance of the week as the attorneys on both sides will fight every point of the case," the Choteau Acantha stated.

Twenty-five witnesses, six of whom were for the defense, were subpoenaed. With two newspapers published in Choteau at the time, everyone was talking about the case taking place in the Teton County Courthouse.

Choteau Montanan publisher C.E. Trescott wrote his take on the trial on March 20. "The case has been on trial during the week. There is an imposing array of legal talent engaged on the trial. County Attorney D.W. Doyle and his able assistant, Thos. H. Pridham, are being assisted in the prosecution by attorneys John G. Bair and Walter Verge of this city. The defense is being looked after by attorney Sidney M. Logan of Kalispell and R. M. Hattersley of Conrad.

"The evidence in the case is practically all circumstantial, and seems to point clearly to the guilt of the accused. The defense, however, does not admit the killing, but yesterday attempted to show by witnesses that Clifford's death might possibly have been caused by a shot from someone other than Dawe, and that the death was due to an accident.

"The defense does not rely, however, for an acquittal, on the theory that Clifford was killed by a stray bullet, but have made a strenuous effort to prove that Dawe was insane at the time of the killing, and therefore not responsible for his acts.

"The case will probably go to the jury for their decision sometime this (Friday) evening."

Choteau Acantha proprietor C.G. Bishop's edition came out on March 25 after the verdict came in, but before getting to that, here's Bishop's take on the case.

"The principal witness for the state, William Bell of Valier, swore to the hearing of the shot fired [something he denied at the coroner's inquest] and to seeing Dawe just before the murder and just after, and the peculiar action at these times. Other witnesses were examined to find a motive for the crime and to prove sanity. No eyewitnesses to the killing were found and the prosecuting [attorneys] were obliged to base their case on circumstantial evidence alone."

The defense attorneys argued that sufficient evidence for conviction was not presented and that if the jury thought that there was sufficient evidence, that the defendant was insane and not responsible for the crime.

"The principal witness for the defense was Mrs. William Dawe, mother of the defendant, who toward the latter part of the trial became unable to bear the strain and was obliged to remain away. Many doctors were called to provide the insanity of Dawe and depositions of doctors who had known the defendant were presented. The defense put up a hard fight and contested every point of the case," Bishop said.

Three doctors and one U.S. Army medical officer in depositions outlined Dawe's path to perdition. Dawe graduated from the Cincinnati (Ohio) College of Medicine and Surgery in 1902.

In summary, when Dawe was 21 or 22 he suffered a long and severe siege from typhoid fever. After the fever left him, he was never the same as he had been before, the attorneys argued. He began the habit of using drugs and he contracted an alcohol habit. He entered a sanitarium for four weeks in 1905 and eight weeks in 1906, with both times unsuccessful. In August 1907 he was committed to the Toledo (Ohio) State Hospital for the insane, was discharged on probation in January 1908, and returned there a month later until April 1908.

Sometime after that he became a first lieutenant in the U.S. Army's Medical Reserve Corps, and was eventually stationed in Plattsburg, New York. During his service he was constantly addicted, and was finally asked to resign. The officer said, "Later I found in five drug stores in Plattsburg, that Dawe during his month's stay had purchased considerable quantities of cocaine hydrochlorate and morphine sulphate at two of them, without authorization."

In December 1910 he was again committed, and was discharged in November 1911.

Dawe came to Montana and was employed as a physician for a ditch contracting company, but he sat down on a very hot stove and burned himself very severely and was fired from the job. He homesteaded, continued drugs, married a young English immigrant, Florence Edge, in Valier, "but then marriage domestic troubles began," the attorneys offered.

That, along with other erratic incidents while intoxicated or drugged, culminated in that fateful day when Chaparral Charley died.

The Dawe file in the courthouse today, while having no transcriptions of the trial testimony, nevertheless, includes a thick, yellowed brief of 45 jury instructions.

The jury had several choices: murder in the first or second degree, manslaughter (voluntary or involuntary), not guilty or not guilty by reason of insanity. The jury had the privilege of fixing the penalty.

Dawe's addictions to drugs and alcohol became a central part of the defense's case. Four physicians provided depositions stating that Dawe appeared to be insane at the time, based on his previous behavior while under the influence, and based on what they had been told by the defense attorneys of the circumstances leading up to Clifford's death from a gunshot wound to the neck.

Under state law at the time, "lunatics and insane persons" were incapable of committing a crime because they could not be guilty of deliberation, premeditation, malice or act with willfulness.

The law presumed every man is sane, but that may be overcome, the instructions stated. It is not necessary that it be established by a preponderance of the evidence that the defendant was insane, "but if you entertain a reasonable doubt as to the sanity at the time of commission, it is your duty to give him the benefit of the doubt and acquit him on grounds of insanity."

Definitions of insanity followed, as did paragraphs on evidence, among other things. An instruction stated, "If you believe beyond a reasonable doubt he committed the crime, and at the time the defendant knew it was wrong, and was mentally capable of choosing either to do it or not do the act, then it is your duty to find him guilty even though you should believe from the evidence that at the time of the commission of the crime he was not entirely and perfectly sane."

The defense's telling of the crime described a man out of control the day of the killing, with drinking to excess and indulging in the use of cocaine or morphine or some kindred drug.

After several incidents in Valier, he was jailed for three hours. While there, he took out a pocketknife and attempted to cut his throat but was prevented by officers. He exhibited frequent and divergent moods, and gave himself over to crying spells.

In justice court that afternoon, (presumably for some infraction having to do with his behavior) he was moody and wept frequently. A hearing was set for the following morning, and he was ordered to return home. He started on the way accompanied by an officer for part of it.

The only complaint Dawe ever made of Clifford was that on one occasion Clifford carried Dawe's wife's suitcase into town for her, (during one of their frequent marital troubles) and that on the forenoon, before leaving town, he said to the officer that he was going to "lick old Charley."

The officer said to him, "You couldn't lick an old man like him." To which Dawe replied, "That's the hell of it."

Dawe proceeded home about eight miles and he passed the place where Charley lived. That evening Charley was found with a bullet hole in the neck penetrating the spinal column, with the defendant bending over him moving his arms up and down in an effort to induce artificial respiration.

The defense never said Dawe did the deed, but if he did, the doctors swore he was insane.

The March 25, 1914, Choteau Acantha said, "After a

continuous deliberation of two days and two nights, the jury in the case of the state vs. Dawe returned a verdict of guilty of manslaughter and left the penalty to be imposed by the court.

"The penalty that is provided by the law is one to 10 years in the penitentiary. The trial of the case took eight days, during which time the courtroom was crowded to capacity and the highest interest manifested throughout."

The Choteau Montanan weighed in on March 27, "It is thought by disinterested persons who have followed the trial closely, that Dawe certainly deserves the maximum penalty. The trial commenced on March 17 and everything possible was done to save the accused from the natural effects of his vicious actions."

The record is silent as to whether Dawe was guilty of voluntary or involuntary manslaughter, "the unlawful killing of a human without malice," in the death of neighbor Charlie Clifford near Valier. The jury declined to impose a penalty and instead, District Judge H.H. Ewing imposed it, which resulted on March 28 in Dawe's getting the maximum sentence of 10 years at hard labor in the penitentiary in Deer Lodge.

The principal witness for the defense was Mrs. William Dawe, mother of the defendant, who toward the latter part of the trial "became unable to bear the strain and was obliged to remain away."

The Acantha reported that Mrs. Dawe went missing during the jury deliberations, but about 12:45 a.m. she was found in the Methodist church between two of the rows of seats, "and since that time has been under the doctor's care because of nervousness caused by the excitement of the trial."

The Choteau Montanan posted after the trial, "Considerable sympathy was 'manufactured' for him by some of the good but mistaken and hysterical women of the town, who attended each session of court, openly expressing sympathy and good will toward the prisoner, even in the presence of the jurors who were sworn to try the case without prejudice or partiality, but who certainly must have been influenced by these actions to a greater or less extent."

Continuing, "The verdict was clearly a compromise one: as it is generally understood that during the balloting, the jurors stood six for conviction of murder and six for acquittal. Those who voted for acquittal were of the opinion that Dawe was insane when the murder was committed."

Dawe's attorneys filed a notice of the intention to move for a new trial, but nothing came of that.

On April 1, Dawe and his wife, Florence, signed the deed to his homestead and conveyed the ranch to his attorney, R. Hattersley, and on April 2 Sheriff McKenzie and J.M. Weaver took Dawe to Deer Lodge along with five other prisoners, a busy term of court, the newspapers noted.

Dawe's mug shot on his prison intake sheet shows a handsome fellow with a distinct "Roman" nose, age 33 and 6.5 inches tall with brown hair and grey eyes. The record noted that he had come to Montana on July 1, 1911, and was a surgeon in the army, but had been more recently employed as a bookkeeper in Valier. His health was listed as "good - morphine fiend."

Dawe's mother and wife never lost faith in the man, as shown by their periodic visits to the prison. In early December 1916 the state Board of Pardons held a hearing on the commutation of Dawe's sentence. Although it was "continued on account of a protest signed by 100 people," Gov. S. Stewart approved the commutation on Dec. 24, 1916. (The people of Valier had raised $250 for the prosecution of the case.)

Dawe kicked his addictions. The three Dawes moved to

Boston, Massachusetts, where Dawe was granted a medical license and by 1920 he was employed as a physician for the U.S. Public Health Service. He was later appointed acting assistant surgeon. The family, including a daughter, born in 1919, moved to Queens, New York, by 1925. Dawe, 56, died on April 1, 1937, and was buried in his native Cincinnati, Ohio.

The Dawe trial made news on one more occasion. William Miller, the Democratic candidate for sheriff, was up for reelection to a two-year term in the fall of 1916, and he compared the county's financial statements from 1914 and 1915 to insinuate that he had saved the county $10,000 ($241,000 in today's dollars) during 1915 compared to the year before.

Choteau Montanan publisher C.E. Trescott could not let that pass. His editorial on Oct. 27, 1916, was headlined "Billy Peddles Bunk." Trescott explained that in 1914 there were two murder trials and two rape cases, all requiring payments to many witnesses and jurors, while no important cases occurred during Miller's term.

"Certainly the sheriff had nothing to do with saying who should or should not attend court as a witness or a juror. He simply served the summonses handed him by the proper officials," Trescott said. Miller won anyway, but two years later he decided not to run for a third term.

22

The Glidden Tour to Glacier

July 18, 25, August 1, 8, 15, 22, 29, 2018

The 1913 Glidden Tour from Minneapolis to Glacier National Park, proclaimed the Sept. 3, 1913, Acantha, "created a new epoch in the national automobile tour, inasmuch as it was the first time that a modern car run of this kind ever penetrated the Rocky Mountains."

Louis W. Hill, board chairman of the Great Northern Railway, and one of the owners of the new Glacier Park Hotel at the park's eastern entrance, had scored a coup in getting the annual auto reliability tour to end at the new hotel. It cost the railway $50,000 to "have the Glidden Tour follow its line this year," the April 24 Big Timber Press reported.

"If a single tour of 50 autos, passing through the country tapped by this road, is worth that amount in advertising and in anticipated results to that road, what would it be worth to Montana and the Yellowstone valley, to secure this great permanent national highway, over which it is estimated from 25 to 50 autos will travel each day," the Press opined.

A year earlier, the locals of Thompson Falls and Murray, Idaho, had sought to get the 1913 auto tour to come their way. "The Minneapolis to coast trip would mean 75 to 100 cars would pass through the towns on the route and the publicity given by one of these trips is immense. It would be a fine thing for this country," reported the Sanders County Ledger. "The field representative was tasked to lay out four routes from coast to coast, which will be transcontinental highways, easily traveled, without undue hardship and in reasonable road time by automobiles."

The annual auto tour traced its roots back to 1904, but Boston millionaire Charles J. Glidden had given it a solid boost by 1906. Glidden and his wife had made a tour of the world in his automobile in 1905, covering 25,000 miles. His interest in reliable autos prompted local communities to spend money on reliable roads as the country left horse-drawn carriages in the barns.

The May 1907 Scientific American reported that with Glidden's financial backing, "The chief touring event in America this year is to be conducted by the American Automobile Association in July. This will be the third annual contest for the Glidden trophy and will start from Cleveland on July 10.

"The route will be through Detroit and Lansing, Michigan, to Chicago; thence south and east to Indianapolis, Columbus, Cincinnati, Pittsburgh, Harrisburg, Philadelphia and New York.

"It is proposed to have only noon and night controls, with two minutes leeway; also to require the cars to make a good average speed behind a pacemaker and not to allow them to use any spare parts except those they carry with them. Besides the Glidden trophy for touring cars (which will this year be awarded to the club which makes the best showing) a trophy has been offered for runabouts and will be awarded to the owner who makes the best performance with his style of car."

The Glidden tour was so well known by March 1909 that Choteau dentist Dr. C.B.J. Stephens used it in his advertisements for the Stephens Automobile Co. he formed with J.W. Walker of Kalispell.

Its Acantha ad displayed a drawing of a REO, a five-passenger touring car that sold for $1,000 with a top being extra, a four-passenger roadster with top for $1,000 and a runabout for $500.

"When you are starting out for a motor trip, short or long, the one thing you want to be sure of is that you will get back without fuss or delay. The record of the REO on the Glidden tours and on ordinary daily tours is splendid for its reliability. Let us prove this to you when our shipment of cars arrive, which will be in only a few days."

Two months later a new REO ad read, "The kind of car which went 140 miles a day through the rough trails of the Glidden Tour for two weeks and finished in such perfect condition that it was chosen to pilot the big four- and six-cylinder Runabouts running off the ties. This kind of car can be safely counted upon to get you 'there and back' any day you go out. The last of the carload is sold. Place your orders now for the next shipment. We are agents for REO, Overland and Franklin Cars."

The American Automobile Association's annual reliability tours, commonly known as the Glidden tours, offered the promise of national publicity for towns along the route.

Commercial clubs vied to have the 50-some Glidden "tourist" cars come through their cities and towns. The tour was not run in 1912 because of a scarcity of participants, but the A.A.A. said it would host one the following year.

A September 1912 Daily Missoulian article reported, "Commercial clubs from Fargo to Helena are cooperating with Missoula in the endeavor to influence the A.A.A. to continue its Glidden tour out through the Northwest in 1913. In a communication received from A.G. Batchelder, chairman of the executive committee of the A.A.A., touching upon this subject, he says: 'We beg to acknowledge receipt of the invitation of all the commercial clubs of western Montana to include Missoula in the 1913 reliability tour. If such an event is conducted wholly or in part over the northern transcontinental route, this matter will be referred to the 1913 tour committee immediately after it is appointed after the annual meeting in December next, and you can rest assured that the claims of your wonderful state will be most carefully considered by that committee. Such a trip would certainly prove a liberal education to many whom have yet to realize the possibilities of the inland empire country.'

"Mr. Batchelder attended the recent Montana Good Roads Congress and while there, was asked to use his influence regarding this tour by the Missoula delegation. He was greatly in love with Montana and said he would work hard for it. A.L. Westgard, the [tour's] pathfinder, also said that he would recommend Missoula be on this reliability tour."

News reports had earlier indicated that the 1913 Glidden tour would follow the now-aborted New Orleans to Detroit route designated in 1912. Boston millionaire and auto enthusiast Charles J. Glidden had, however, driven the route by himself and his account reported "terrible roads." He also criticized the 1912 tour planners, who had forgotten to notify the hotels and eateries along the route that the tour had been cancelled. The hoteliers had bought extra provisions and had hired extra help at great expense, it was said.

Best to choose another part of the country, and that is when Louis W. Hill, the board chairman of the Great Northern Railway had an opening to promote Glacier National Park and his new 61-room Glacier Park Hotel set to open on June 15 at the park's eastern entrance north of the Midvale (now East Glacier Park) railroad station. The park had opened three years earlier with only tents, and a few private hotels for accommodations. The new hotel had cost the railway $200,000 to build.

In April 1913, the A.A.A. announced it had chosen

the 1,233-mile-long Minneapolis to Glacier National Park route.

The Washington Times reported, "Louis W. Hill, chairman of the board of directors of the GN Railway, an enthusiastic motorist, and an entrant in the tour, has agreed to run a palatial 'automobile hotel train' without a single paid fare, in order that the contestants may have adequate eating and sleeping accommodations en route. The newspaper correspondents 'covering' the tour will get out a daily paper each day of the tour, a printing plant being carried in one of the baggage cars of the automobile train."

Speed would not be the primary object, but time limits were set and repairs on the way, any car damage sustained and lateness would garner penalties. While in the earlier tours the drivers could only use the spare parts they could carry, in 1913, the A.A.A. relaxed the rules to allow for repairs with the spare parts carried in a train car designated for it. "This train will be made up of Pullman sleepers, dining cars, observation cars and baggage cars. It will be a veritable traveling hotel for the accommodation of the tourists and will stop at every night control along the route for the accommodation of the travelers," the Williston, North Dakota, Graphic reported.

The Glidden tourists would leave Minneapolis on their nine-day westward journey to the "American Alps" on July 11.

Meanwhile, the GN Railway office sent personal invitations to return to the park to visitors who registered at the Glacier National Park entrance the previous year.

Twenty-eight cars started from Minneapolis on July 11, 1913, in a drizzling rain in hopes of winning the Glidden trophy in the American Automobile Association's nine-day National Reliability Tour that would end under the arch at the new Glacier Park Hotel.

Three auto manufacturers entered driving teams — three teams in Metz Model 22 roadsters, the K-R-I-T Motor Co. offered three light runabouts; and R.W. Munzer and Sons Co. entered two Hupmobiles, nicknamed the "little diamond." The rest were individual owners from Minnesota and North Dakota, save one or two. Great Northern Railway Chairman Louis W. Hill started the race in a Packard, and Dr. J.D. Parks, the president of the Duluth Auto Club, entered the tour in a four-year-old Locomobile.

"One of the features of the tour this year will be the entry of a car owned and driven by an Indian. Long Time Sleeping, a member of the Blackfeet Indian tribe whose reservation home is alongside Glacier National Park will be the Indian to take the trip," the newspapers reported. He and other tribal members had accompanied Hill to New York on a publicity tour for the park a few months earlier. An unnamed Sioux Indian entered the tour so that more than one tribe was represented, the news said.

The actual running time from the Hotel Radisson in Minneapolis to Glacier was eight days with Sunday, July 13, designated as a day of rest. The night stops and distances between them in miles were: Alexandria, Minnesota, 144.41; Fargo, North Dakota, 123.8; Devil's Lake, 194.6; Minot, 135.6; Williston, 136.8; Glasgow, Montana, 163.8; Havre, 158.1; and Glacier National Park, 178.

"This is being made more of a society event than a grueling contest, the only requirement being to get into the control on time. The daily mileage is easy and comfortable," the Williston Graphic opined.

The news said Hill equipped a "hotel" train to run just ahead of the motorists, to stop at noon controls for lunch in the dining cars, and parking at the night controls, so that the "autoists" could occupy the sleeping cars. The train carried more than 200 people, and besides the "hotel," it had a barbershop, repair shop and everything found in a city. Expert drivers drove the cars and one of each car's passengers was a mechanic from the auto factory where the car was made.

A pilot car was first, followed 15 minutes later by the pacemaker, occupied by the committee in charge. Hill drove the first car, but he never intended to do the long run and left his vehicle after a short time. He would appear in the news again at a stop in Popular.

After the first day to Alexandria, the tour followed the Northwest Trail to Fargo; then made a northward turn to Grand Forks, then west following the general line of the railway. From Havre it was a direct line to the park. After running into and through the park, the tourists were invited to visit Kalispell to attend a meeting of the Montana Good Roads Congress.

Hill also had something special planned — a blaze of glory finish. "The illuminated panoramic mountain spectacle [red, green or white and blue-colored fireworks] will be flashed upon the approaching motorists when the pilot car is crossing the Montana prairie within 40 miles of the range."

And in a concession to the Montana commercial clubs that had pressed for their towns to be on the route, the news reported, "After reaching the park, numerous side trips will be taken to places of interest in that section. Indian reservations will be visited and tribal ceremonies witnessed. The tourists will be encouraged to return over the roads through Missoula and Butte or Helena to Livingston and Gardiner where they may leave their cars and make stage trips in the Yellowstone National Park."

On June 22, a week after its official opening date, Glacier Park Hotel hosted more than 360 excursionists, the Columbian newspaper reported. "Seven passenger coaches comfortably filled with Columbia Falls and Kalispell people attended and took part in the opening of the big hotel at Glacier Park, located at the eastern entrance of Glacier National Park last Sunday." They helped to "break in" the hotel staff, for the coming Glidden tourists.

The Glidden tourists set out on July 11. Glacier National Park had opened on June 15, although the biggest crowd did not arrive until June 22, in a special train packed with people from Columbia Falls and Kalispell, there being no road over Marias Pass as yet.

J.M. McGaughy, assistant general freight and passenger agent for the Great Northern Railway Co., invited previous park guests via a letter in early June.

"Dear Sir: Glacier National Park will be open to tourists on June 15 and will remain open until Oct. 1. Arrangements have been made to handle tourists via automobiles, stages or horses. At the opening of the season we will place a large number of 60-horsepower, seven-passenger touring cars in service between Glacier Park station and Two Medicine Camp; daily four-horse stage service between St. Mary's Camp and Many Glacier Camp (Lake McDermott.) The stage rates will be $1.50 one way, $2.50 round trip between Glacier Park Hotel and Two Medicine Camp and $2.50 one way, $5 round trip between St. Mary's Camp and Many Glacier Camp, regardless of the number of passengers.

"The new hotel at the entrance of Glacier Park station has been completed with a capacity of 200. We have also added Swiss chalets to our various camps and with a stage between St. Mary's and Many Glacier Camp, it will make it possible for many who did not last year make the trip, to visit the Iceberg Lake and Swift Current Pass which are very beautiful.

"Stages will also be operated between Glacier Park station and Cut Bank Camp. We have just launched on St.

Mary's Lake a large new pleasure craft, capacity 125 persons, which will make the trip from St. Mary's Going to the Sun Camp, formerly called 'The Narrows.' The scenery at that point is most beautiful.

"Additional facilities have been provided for handling of tourists via the western entrance at Belton by stage to Lake McDonald, thence across Lake McDonald to Glacier Hotel. The government has built a very fine road from Glacier Hotel to Sperry glacier. A great many improvements have been made since last year, which we feel will enable us to take care of visitors with a greater degree of comfort.

"The records kept at the entrance show that you visited the park last year. If you expect to visit again this year or if any of your friends want to visit the park this season, we will be very glad to send upon application our latest literature containing many new and beautiful photograph reproductions as well as full explanations regarding rates, trips, time, etc."

The special train that delivered more than 300 excursionists from Columbia Falls and Kalispell to the Glacier Park Hotel took them back across the Continental Divide at 6 p.m.

The news report summarized their visit, "Here was found the strangest mixture of humanity that one could ask for. The English nobleman, with monocle at his eye, the American easterner dressed in his large checked wearing apparel, the average ordinary pleasure-seeking gentleman, the [resident] Indian and gaily bedecked [wife and baby], in fact, every nationality and character in life, almost, filled the vast lobby, corridors and verandas.

"The interior of the big hotel is beyond description; one must visit and inspect to realize the wonderful piece of architecture, which has cost the Great Northern Railway Co. over $200,000 to build."

Wanting to tap into the Glidden tour outstanding national publicity (costing not less than $2,500 and covering more than 500 newspapers throughout the United States) Clem Bowers of the Choteau Garage and Machine Co., during the first week of July, went to Great Falls and returned that evening with two new Hupmobiles. "The Hups are excellent cars and are gradually winning their way in public favor in this section," the Acantha said. William Hodgskiss, the owner of the Choteau House, bought one of the seven-passenger Hupmobiles the following week.

"The machine is certainly a beauty," the Acantha stated.

The news said Mr. and Mrs. Chas. McDonald of Choteau would go to Midvale on July 18 to see the Glidden auto tourists. Local blacksmith Charles LePage was hired to be one of the men who would light the fireworks set up on the mountain tops when the Glidden tourists arrived.

The Glidden Tour across Minnesota, North Dakota and Montana in July 1913 was a test of auto reliability.

A month earlier on June 15, a $1,500 Mitchell "Moose" four-cylinder pathfinding car had left Minneapolis to make the 1,233-mile-long run to Glacier National Park, or "Uncle Sam's Switzerland of America," hoping to average about 20 miles an hour on the gravel roads, while making sure the route was properly signed.

Driver Frank Zirbes gained fame in 1910 by driving a car from New York to San Francisco without changing a tire. He also traveled by auto throughout Europe. Scout C.A. Stedman was the official pathfinder who dropped confetti to mark the route. Passenger Wm. S. Forman was a spokesman for the tour sponsor, the American Automobile Association.

"The men were pretty well tired out when they reached Grand Forks about 10 o'clock last night," the local Evening News reported. "They left Fergus Falls at eight o'clock yesterday morning. A short distance out of Barnesville they ran into a windstorm and hardly had they got through that, [when] they hit a rainstorm and from Barnesville to Fargo the roads were exceedingly bad. After leaving Fargo, they made the run to Crookston at a good rate. After having dinner there, the party continued to this city. They spent the night here and left early this morning for Devil's Lake."

"Rope, shovel, ax and other touring equipment are being carried by the Mitchell Moose as driver Zirbes has had some experience of many years blazing trails and doesn't take any chances of spending the night in some hole where there is no bottom to the road. 'As long as there is a footing to be had,' said he, 'the Moose will take us anywhere,'" wrote the Dillon Examiner.

On July 2, the Examiner published a report sent from Malta on June 30. "Real joyous pathfinding has been the lot of the crew of the Mitchell Moose car which is laying out the route for the 1913 national A.A.A. tour Minneapolis to Glacier Park. The Montana end of the route, as found by Scout Stedman, has been a succession of swamps and flat alkali mudholes. Wherever the wheels of the powerful Moose could get traction, the car pulled out bravely, but when the 'no bottom' spots were encountered, Indian braves and their cow ponies came to the rescue with ropes.

"Motorists along the route of the pathfinder are on the qui vive [on the alert] because of the importance and size of this national A.A.A. touring event. ... Many women, both as entrants and passengers, will participate in the event and every arrangement possible will be made for their comfort. It is to be hoped that the same luck won't befall the cars in the tour, as befell the Moose.

"Because of the quicksand and mudholes met with between Rugby and this point, [Malta] the crew of the car have slept in barns, eaten at all hours and done considerable traveling after dark. It's all in the game of pathfinding, however, and knowing their mount would respond to any demand made, reasonable or otherwise, long hours and high mileage, considering conditions have been the rule.

"If dry weather prevails before the tour starts from Minneapolis, July 11, the Fort Peck Indian Reservation roads will be much better than when the Moose covered them. The Indian entertainment planned will be hugely enjoyed by easterners."

The pathfinder arrived in Shelby on July 1, but no news reports chronicle its arrival at the Glacier Park Hotel. All news now focused on the July 11-19 American Automobile Association's National Reliability Tour, or Glidden Tour.

"Although this famous touring event has lost some of its prestige, its running is still followed by motorists in all sections of the country and the winner is declared the premier road driver of the country," wrote Washington Times sports writer Harry Ward.

"In selecting Glacier National Park for the objective of their tour the Glidden officials have made a wise selection. This is one of the few national parks where automobiling is allowed in the park. The Great Northern Railway Co. has expended thousands of dollars in beautifying the park and has built at its own expense a splendid auto road, 35 miles in length, from Glacier Park, the town at the east entrance to the big playgrounds, to St. Mary's Lake, one of the grand beauty spots," the Williston Graphic reported.

On July 10, 1913, 28 (some reports say 30 or 32) Glidden Tour drivers saw that their machines were in perfect shape and examined their equipment to see that it was complete and in readiness for the long run from Minneapolis to Glacier National Park.

They got their numbers for their cars and badges for themselves, guests and drivers.

The itinerary of the tour was set but would be slightly changed, later news reports show. Friday, July 11, leave Twin Cities, noon control, St. Cloud; night control, Alexandria. Saturday, July 12, noon control, Fergus Falls; night control, Fargo. Sunday, July 13, all day stop in Fargo. Monday, July 14, leave Fargo, noon control, Crookston; night control, Grand Forks. Tuesday, July 15, noon control, Larimore; night control, Devil's Lake. Wednesday, July 16, noon control, Rugby; night control, Minot. Thursday, July 17, noon control, Stanley; night control, Williston. Friday, July 18, noon control, Popular; night control, Glasgow. Saturday, July 19, noon control, Malta; night control, Havre. Sunday July 20, noon control, Shelby; end tour at Glacier Park.

The Great Northern Railway Co. equipped a hotel train to run just ahead of the motorists, stopping at noon controls so they could have access to the dining cars, and parking at the night controls, so that the participants could occupy the sleeping cars at night.

After the train reached Devil's Lake, only 25 autos arrived, all in by dark, but the news reports noted they had had "a rather hard time between here and Fargo as the rains had put the roads in bad conditions in places. They simply had to plow through mud. However, they seemed to all be enjoying themselves, and after a good night's rest here, they went on their way rejoicing."

At Popular, "the Indians gave a big demonstration for the benefit of the visitors. They took Louis W. Hill of the Great Northern Railway out of his car, dressed him up as a regular Indian, put him on a horse and had him lead the procession through town," the Williston Graphic reported.

On Saturday night about 6 o'clock the first cars of the Glidden tour arrived at the Glacier Park Hotel, one day late, the Acantha reported. The first, second and fourth cars arriving were the Metz team, and the third was a K-R-I-T.

"The Boston team represented by three Metz cars was the only team that finished with a perfect score, a record which, when taken in connection with the almost perfect condition of the Metz cars upon arrival, is most wonderful.

"The major portion of cars that failed to arrive at termination died in heavy two days of gumbo mud experienced on July 11 and 12 just after leaving Minneapolis.

"The winners of the cup, the Boston team, stated to a representative of the Acantha that the roads through Montana were excellent and the only trouble experienced was on the Cut Bank hill.

"The accommodations at the hotel were absolutely taxed, it being impossible for the management to furnish rooms and beds for the numerous visitors. The special train of Pullmans that accompanied the Glidden tourists to Glacier Park was placed at the disposal of guests who were unable to secure accommodations at the hotel, and even then it was necessary for many to sleep on benches in the depot.

"This event has proved a great advertisement for Montana, and Louie Hill is to be complimented upon the success of this large undertaking," the Acantha reported.

The Columbia Falls paper said, "Twenty four cars reached Glacier station Saturday evening, and a more tired, exhausted and nerve-racked crowd of men would be hard to find. The strain of the long run was evident upon the faces of every contestant and one driver had to be lifted from his car at the finish of the run. Most of the visitors took first to the plunge bath [in the hotel basement] and then to bed, where they remained until late Sunday morning.

"Louis Hill is with the party and will remain for some time within the park, making his headquarters in his own teepee, erected by his Indian friends near the big hotel."

The 1913 Glidden Tour ended at the Glacier Park Hotel

on July 19, but news reports including praise and advertisements for the various makes of automobiles lasted for months.

In the aftermath, Louis W. Hill, the chairman of the Great Northern Railway Co., made grand plans for expansion of the 61-room Glacier Park Hotel by adding a 110-room annex, among other additions. And park officials agreed to make "wide, 'boulevard trails' over the great divide in three places — Gunsight, Swift Current and Peigan passes. This assures safe horseback travel over the top of the continent three different ways," the news noted.

The Acantha reported, "The 1913 Glidden Tour from Minneapolis to Glacier National Park created a new epoch in the national automobile tour, inasmuch as it was the first time that a modern car run of this kind ever penetrated the Rocky Mountains.

"Thirty cars started from Minneapolis on July 11 in a drizzling rain, and all except two, finished in front of the Glacier Park Hotel after a run of 1,233 miles through three states — Minnesota, North Dakota and Montana."

At the finish, C.A. Munzer, driving one of the Hupmobiles, which won the runabout prize, "collapsed from a nervous prostration as he drew up in front of the AAA officials with only a fraction of a minute to spare.

"The tour has already proved one of the greatest incentives to good road building in the history of the Northwest, nearly $1,000,000 in road repairs having been made to make the national event a success. The Great Northern Railway transcontinental automobile route from the Twin Cities to Seattle now is an assurance."

The Metz trio won the Glidden trophy and Dr. L.A. Park, driving a four-year-old Locomobile, won the touring car prize, the last one awarded because no more Glidden tours were staged after 1913.

An Abbeville, Louisiana, news report, probably paid for by the auto manufacturer, praised the Hupmobile.

"On crippled rims, with but a bare minute to spare, the second Hupmobile 32 entered in the 1913 Glidden Tour, dashed under the massive redwood arch that framed the picturesque finish of the tour. Twelve minutes before, the other Hupmobile entry was brought in the final control by a safe margin, this making for the Hups, perfect scores.

"The tour put the cars to the most severe test, when for the first three days the going was awful from rain and mud.

"Leaving Fargo on the third day, they went through 90 miles of the worst gumbo ever found, and the crippled pacemaker caused every car to slow down to 10 miles per hour. Then it was that the Hupmobile made a showing that stood as a record for the trip. Every radiator, except those of the Hups, boiled from two to four times, but the Hup radiators never took on water anywhere during the trip out of control."

An Omaha Daily Bee ad noted, "Both the Glidden and Minneapolis News trophies were captured by the Metz '22' roadster. This demonstrates that it is possible to build a thoroughly good car to sell at a conspicuously low price. The team of three Metz stock cars was the only team to maintain a perfect score for the entire eight days. They completely vanquished their competitors." The Metz 22 cost $475, completely equipped.

"The Metz team of regular stock cars was last to leave noon control on the last day of the tour, passed all those ahead, caught the pacemaker 10 miles from the finish and crowded him over the last mountain range, finishing the last lap of the tour with 20 minutes to spare."

The fireworks or "illumination of the Rockies" so extensively advertised was not staged, the reason being that no powder arrived, the Acantha reported. Among those attending from Choteau to watch the tour finish were: Alex Burrell, George Burrell, John W. Moore, Chas. LePage, Mr. and Mrs. E.E. Leech and daughter, Florence; Mr. and Mrs. C.S. McDonald, Mr. and Mrs. Jay Cowell, T.C. Spaulding, Tom Larson and Julius Hirshberg.

In October the news reported that more than 11,000 tourists had visited the park between June and September, "setting another record for all the rest of Uncle Sam's playgrounds, nearly twice as many as last year. And yet the Rocky Mountain park is only in the third year of its existence. Cheap transportation and low, hotel rates, government officials declare, are making Glacier National Park the most popular people's resort in the country."

— 23 —
Camp Fire Girls
March 30, 2016

The first mention of the Camp Fire Girls in Choteau's newspapers was in spring 1917, when the named group of 16 young women volunteered to help grow vegetables, along with other groups, on vacant lots in Choteau as part of the war effort.

A national organization had been around informally since 1910, but it formally became a sister organization to the Boy Scouts of America on March 17, 1912. It is not clear when the group in Choteau was formed.

"The Camp Fire Girls, with their guardian, [Kate Hall] enjoyed a very pleasant three days camping out at the McDonald ranch last week. ... Four cars took the party out and with Mrs. McDonald's assistance, located them in a very pretty spot on the banks of McDonald Creek. Wading, swimming, fishing, climbing, hiking, became the order of the day, and when the heat made these pastimes fall a little, the McDonalds' piano, graphaphone and candy kitchen made the time pass quickly and pleasantly. Some of the girls won honors in camp cooking, camp craft and photography, which made the outing doubly worthwhile to them. All the crowd was ready to proclaim our first camping out a success and the McDonalds royal hosts."

The Choteau Montanan published a 500-word diary of one of the girls who went on the campout that August 1917. It said in part, "About seven we reached McDonald's ranch. In crossing the creek our Ford got stuck. More power was put on, but power and noise didn't do any good. We girls got out and by pulling on the rope, which was tied on the axle; we helped a Ford to ford the creek. An hour's waiting brought out the rest of our bunch in the cars of Messrs. Guthrie, Cole and Sturgeon. It was funny, but Mr. Cole's car got stuck in the creek, too. He said he was a good driver but there was a 'hole in the creek.'

"The first day was spent in walking and exploring and, as we were all tired, [we] turned in early to bed, and turned some more when we got into bed. I mean those of us that could turn for we were quite crowded, sleeping nine to one bed and seven in the other.

"I never thought there were so many noises at night, the river murmured incessantly and once we were sure we heard something awful, but we learned later it was only a cow tripping over some of our belongings. Mrs. Hall slept in our tent so we really tried to go to sleep, but those in the other tent were just awful. They told ghost stories until Mrs. Hall threatened to throw cold water on them if they didn't keep still."

In November 1917, the Camp Fire Girls assumed the support of a French war orphan, which required them to raise $100 per year for the orphan's schooling in Grenoble, France, clothing and care. Her name was given, variously, as Katherine Brach and Catherine Brash. The girls in Choteau hosted minstrel shows and socials with a $.25 admission toward the effort.

The Camp Fire Girls's "15 minutes of fame" came in August 1920 when the Great Falls Tribune published the guardian, Mrs. Thyra Haugen's journal, complete with the girls' group photograph, of a weeklong campout. The Choteau Acantha published one of the girl's journals of the trip at the same time.

The Tribune introduced them, "Those who think there

is no adventure or fun in a week's outing in the mountains will do well to peruse the diary of the Pottawatomie Camp Fire Girls of Choteau, the members of which organization recently spent a week camping on the south fork of the Teton River near Ear Mountain ranger station, one of the most picturesque spots in northwestern Montana.

"Their first trouble started when those riding to camp in one of Henry Ford's masterpieces had to get out and push it up a hill. During the week they had all kinds of accidents, such as falling into the creek, spilling dirt and ashes into the beans, when they tried to open the bean hole, and various other things."

They are great reads — "feel good" narratives of what was a simpler time of no war, no Depression, no 1964 flood to change the Teton River Canyon forever, and no electronic devices to dampen social interactions.

The Camp Fire Girls likely reached their zenith in Choteau in 1927 with 40 members, although units were also in Dutton and Fairfield.

There were "plans for reorganization" in 1931, and it worked for a time, then another revival was attempted in 1939, while the group in Fairfield appears to have been running until at least 1962. "Interest waned when it became difficult to secure enough leaders," the Acantha said. ▧

Outfitters in 1933

Choteau was labeled the "gateway" to the game regions of the Rocky Mountains, in a Jan. 29, 1933, Acantha edition. The term is now used to promote the town.

"The Lewis and Clark National Forest, almost at our door, is credited with being the best game forest in the United States. In the region south, west and north of Choteau the U.S. Forest Service has made an estimate of 5,000 elk, and this same region also claims the greatest population of mountain goats, mountain sheep, moose, deer, bear, lynx, beaver and other wild animals of any like area in the world," the article explained.

The promotion continued, "It is largely on account of this game that the dude ranches, or as they are more politely called 'guest ranches,' have come into existence and licensed guides have made their appearance. But even in the closed season and in the summertime, the operators of these ranches conduct camping, fishing and sightseeing trips into the heart of the Rockies. Automobile roads are piercing farther into this wilderness and are making such areas as Sun River, Teton River and Ford Creek available to those who cannot afford a pack outfit or do not have the time."

What followed was a brief description of the best known of those ranches and recreational resorts at that time, notably during the Depression, when customers would be sorely needed.

Pendroy-based Chick Grimsley's camp was in the Black-leaf Canyon west of Bynum. He used it as a base for big game hunting, fishing and sightseeing trips. "Shots at bear in the spring and elk in season are guaranteed. Summer trips afford opportunities for photos of elk, moose, sheep, deer and other wildlife. Trout include rainbow, cutthroat and Dolly Varden; also whitefish. Trips may be made through rugged country in which the Continental Divide is crossed three or four times daily at elevations of from 6,000 to 10,000 feet. Forest Service telephones within easy reach. Saddle horses and pack outfits."

J.L. Gleason and Kenneth Gleason's Circle Eight Ranch was "located on the site of an old Indian village," and on the South Fork of the Teton River 26 miles from Choteau.

"Fishing, big game hunting in season, swimming, horseback riding, mountain climbing, rodeos and pack trips afford vacation diversion in the heart of the Rocky Mountains only a few miles from Glacier National Park. No poisonous insects or snakes. Elevation, 5,000 feet. Meals, cabins, experienced guides and gentle horses. Good automobile road. Fine spring water, home grown vegetables, fresh milk and cream, shower baths. Many beautiful lakes and streams that have been well stocked with fish."

The Twin Lakes camp was located 23 miles west of Choteau along Teton Canyon Road. The camp was about two miles from the canyon and by two lakes, which gave rise to the name. "Cabins neatly furnished, cooking privileges if desired, dancing pavilion, electric lights, swimming, fishing, horses; also dining room service. A pretty spot and well managed by Mr. and Mrs. D.M. Powell."

Iver Lestrud and Joe White operated the Deep Canyon Ranch on the North Fork of the Teton. "They enjoy general popularity and have a fine string of horses. They cater to recreationalists generally in the summer time and to big game hunting in the fall and winter."

The Baker guest ranch was at the junction of the Middle and North forks of the Teton River about 24 miles northwest of Choteau. It was reached by the "new Forest Service road. Hunting, fishing and camping trips. Saddle horses and pack outfits trained for the mountains. Comfortable cabins and wholesome meals with special reference to Sunday dinners. Trips to suit riding ability and convenience of guests. Write Jack Baker, Choteau."

Other camps included Dupuyer-based registered guide Hugh Arbuckle who operated the Lazy Pine Tree Ranch in the Birch Creek Canyon 52 miles north of Choteau, Ray Gibler's camp on the south side of the Teton River near the forks, and Bill Allum's camp near the mouth of the canyon on the North Fork. He had a cabin on Route Creek.

The article concluded, "The encroachment of modern life with its rapid means of travel, the irrigation ditches and canals, and a diversity of other things that mitigate against wildlife shall not deplete this great natural resource and cheat us out of what should be every man's heritage, and woman's, too — the privilege of outdoor recreation."

— 25 —
Plane Crash
April 3, 10, 2019

The Malmstrom Aero Club's red and cream Mooney Mark 20 disappeared on a flight from Great Falls to Boeing Field in Seattle on Friday, Sept. 1, 1961.

The Acantha published news of the plane on Sept. 21. "Missing Airplane Found by Hunters at Chinese Wall. A private plane, missing since Sept. 1 from Malmstrom Air Force Base, Great Falls, was found Wednesday by goat hunters from Klick's camp at Sun River.

"The wreckage was discovered near the South Fork of Rock Creek, having hit the Chinese Wall, and was reported to local officials. All three occupants, M/Sgt. Alton P. Kessey of Malmstrom, who piloted the craft; John A. Waite, a Boeing Aircraft Co. employee, Seattle, and Douglas R. Mendall [Mendell], manager of a Great Falls trailer court, were dead.

"Teton County Sheriff Al Peterson notified the Flathead County Sheriff's Office as the wreckage is in Flathead County.

"On Wednesday, Sept. 6, organized search was called off, but all specific leads were checked out, with extensive activity in the Mullan Pass area. However, hope faded for the men in the lost plane. Search planes from Missoula, Severson Air Activities on Gore Hill, Helena and from Malmstrom joined in the search."

The Union Bulletin of Walla Walla, Washington, reported the story on the same day, with a few more details. "Malmstrom AFB officers were notified Wednesday night of the hunters' discovery last Sunday. They hiked out to report their find. ... Flathead County Sheriff Richard Walsh and Coroner Sol Catron, both of Kalispell, planned to leave for the area Thursday on a horseback and hiking trip they said might take them at least six days."

The Flathead Courier in Polson on Sept. 28, 1961, provided an additional detail about Kessey.

"Flyer Finds Chinese Wall As Fate Plays Ironic Trick. About a month ago M/Sgt. Alton P. Kessey of Malmstrom AFB, Great Falls, reported to Polson airport authorities that he had spotted what appeared to be airplane wreckage atop a peak in the Swan range.

"Kessey and an Air Force captain had flown a civilian craft to Polson from Great Falls. They had crossed over rugged mountainous terrain including the Bob Marshall Wilderness area in which the Chinese Wall is a famous landmark.

"The wall is a huge perpendicular rock formation that juts through the timbered, mountainous country in which there are no roads ... only big game animal trails.

"The Air Force sergeant could not say whether or not he flew over the Chinese Wall. From the meager information he did give, airport authorities decided he must have been referring to Swan Peak in the wreckage report.

"Ironically, less than a week later, Sgt. Kessey found the Chinese Wall. He and two passengers, John A. Waite and Douglas R. [Mendell], both of Seattle, in a Mooney Mark 20 aircraft bound from Great Falls to Seattle in turbulent, icy weather crashed into it at the head of Rock Creek.

"Goat hunters stumbled onto the wreckage and bodies a week ago Sunday. It was Wednesday of last week before they got word of their grisly discovery to authorities. Flathead County Sheriff Dick Walsh and Coroner Sol Catron packed in Thursday of last week to bring out the bodies."

Kessey was 37, Waite, 30; and Mendell, 26. On Oct. 12, Coroner Catron filed death certificates indicating that the crash was in the southeast quarter of the southwest quarter of Section 4, Township 22 North, Range 12 West. This is a location that is northwest of Salt Mountain on the Continental Divide that is the Teton/Flathead county boundary. Catron wrote on each certificate, "Crushed body, airplane accident. Airplane iced in flight and spun into granite wall of Chinese Wall." He added to each document that the bodies were "still in crashed airplane. Removal of body will be made when weather conditions permit."

As it happens, the Chinese Wall is made from the Madison Limestone formation, and is not made of granite.

Catron may have waited until spring to retrieve the bodies, but eventually, Kessey was buried in Jefferson Barracks National Cemetery, Lemay, Missouri; and Mendell in Kettering, Ohio. Waite's remains were sent to Bellevue, Washington, to be cremated.

The plane crash might have been forgotten but the late *Acantha* Senior Citizens News writer Grace Duffey in 1976 added an interesting "rest of the story."

On Oct. 14, 1976, she wrote a column that is here written verbatim. Note that Duffey's story has a few details that are different from the above account, and clarifications are noted with brackets.

"Would you like to hear how the Yogo sapphire set in a ring on the third finger of my right hand happens to have a slight nick on its prism?

"Early in September 1961, the pilot, an employee of Boeing at Seattle, and a sergeant from Malmstrom AFB took off from Great Falls in a plane owned by a private flying club. Their destination was Seattle. The sergeant was a close friend of Sgt. Lloyd Cannon. The day before departure, Sgt. Cannon had entrusted the sergeant with a box of precious stones he had collected from all over the world. They were to be appraised by a Seattle gemologist.

"Shortly after takeoff, the weather forecasters reported a severe blizzard raging in the vicinity of the Chinese Wall. The airport authorities tried to make immediate contact with the pilot, but to no avail. The hours became days and the days turned into weeks, without a single word from the missing plane.

"Three weeks had passed when Bill Anderson, his two sons, Andy and Art, Sgt. Cannon and Jack Duffey [Grace's husband] left with a long string of pack horses for a hunting trip in the vicinity of White River and the Chinese Wall. Sgt. Cannon was anxious to know what had happened to his friend and to the precious stones. The hunting party kept a sharp eye out for sight of the downed plane, but saw nothing along the trail. After several days of hunting, it was time for Andy and Art to get back to attend college and high school. Bill accompanied them back to Choteau and then returned with their horses and more supplies.

"As he neared the Chinese Wall, he noticed a party of hunters from Klick's Guest Ranch searching for something. They had noticed a shiny metallic object protruding from the side of the mountain. It turned out to be the nose of the missing plane. One body hung part way out of the plane; the others were on the ground and had been worked over by wild animals and weather. As soon as Sgt. Cannon was notified, he rode back and identified the serial number as being the one assigned to that plane. They made the long ride to a telephone, where he informed the base and airport authorities of the discovery.

"Since the accident occurred in Lewis and Clark County, [it was actually in Flathead County west of Salt Mountain] the investigating party of the sheriff's office in Helena [Kalispell] made the inspection. They could only surmise that the pilot had attempted to turn back when the storm was causing zero visibility and the plane crashed into the side of the Chinese Wall. As they were examining the interior, one officer noticed a duffle bag far back on the floor of the plane. He was able to bring it out intact. They were astonished to find numerous pillboxes containing precious stones stuffed here and there within the clothing. The FBI suspected smuggling was involved, confiscated the jewels, and sent them to Tiffany's in New York for appraisal. It was then that Sgt. Cannon learned that although some of the jewels were missing, those remaining were worth far more than he had anticipated. Eventually, he received the jewels.

"One of the Yogo sapphires had a tiny nick in it. He gave me the stone set in the ring I am now wearing. It was a memento of the tragic happening. But to me it is more than a memento. It is a remembrance of the beautiful friendship we enjoyed with the Cannons while they were at the base, a friendship that we hope will last during our lifetimes.

"Since I am limited as to writing space, I am unable to give the minute details of this occurrence. If I were to give it a title it would have to be, 'The Day Jewels Rained Down on the Mountain.'"

— 26 —

Tragedy on the Plains: Blackfeet Commemorate Massacre

January 31, 2018

Something terrible happened on Jan. 23, 1870, in our neighboring community to the north, and Jan. 23, 2018, marked the 24th annual commemoration of that 148-year-old event.

Lewis and Clark may have dubbed the stream they explored in 1806, the Marias River, but the Blackfeet Tribe named it the Bear River in the pre-contact era. The 2018 Bear River Commemoration in the Blackfeet Community College's student commons on Jan. 23 was an invitation to revisit the Bear River Massacre, which non-Indians have labeled the Baker Massacre and the Massacre on the Marias.

On Jan. 23, 1870, the U.S. Army encountered Heavy Runner's band on the south banks of the Marias and killed at least 173 Indians — the tribal members say more than 200 — mostly elders, women and children of the well-known friendly chief. The soldiers had been looking for Mountain Chief's band, known to harbor some wanted suspects, but satisfied themselves that any strike was good enough, the historical records say.

The events leading up to the massacre are the stuff of Montana history, and specific details are disputed, but what the Blackfeet know is that the U.S. government never apologized nor has it compensated the survivors or their descendants for their losses. The survivors were left to their own devices after the Army confiscated their horses and took or burned their supplies and buffalo robes in below-zero weather.

It was a turning point for the Blackfeet in their relations with the whites, and it has remained a part of their cultural history passed down to the current fifth generation of those survivors who understand that its memory has affected them as surely as the Holocaust affected Jews and their descendants or that 9-11 will affect generations of those families.

The commemoration included a welcome by Termaine Edmo, the BCC Student Senate president and a survivor's fifth generation descendant, and an opening prayer by Betty Little Plume. Iva Croff, the BCC division chairwoman of Liberal Arts and Piikani Studies, presented a historical overview of the massacre and Browning School teacher Matthew Johnson explained the effects of historical trauma. During the day, BCC's Medicine Spring Library displayed dozens of documents, oral histories and other resources about the massacre and a group participated in a drum dedication after it was strung with a new horsehide.

When the commemorations began years ago, the community was invited to travel on private land to an overlook near where the massacre occurred. However, concern for the kill site — the actual site is also disputed — added with no current agreement with the private landowner, led to a decision to only visit en masse every four years the northside bluffs on public land managed by the Bureau of Reclamation. (A visit in 2020 marked the 150th anniversary of the event.)

The Google map app says the trip from Choteau to Browning is a little more than an hour. Back in 1870, the government had an agency just three miles north of Choteau where the Indians of the region visited to receive annuities promised by treaty, medical care from the agency doctor, and goods from the nearby trading post.

Consider that on Jan. 1, 1870, Heavy Runner and other chiefs met with government officials at the agency. They asked the chiefs to turn over the Indian suspects who murdered Malcolm Clarke in the Prickly Pear Canyon. When that did not happen, the hunt from Fort Shaw commenced, with the result that instead of the suspects' band, the Army met Heavy Runner's band, with only a few warriors at "home." The band was suffering from smallpox. Since the Blackfeet were reputed to be the fiercest warriors in the region, Croff argued, it would have been impossible for the small force to fend off able-bodied warriors. Instead they shot innocents.

Traveling U.S. Highway 89 north has somewhat changed since 1870. Huge snowdrifts along the westside borrow pit north of Two Medicine River on the reservation are evidence of the fierce winds there. Now out on the plains again, there are no trees, just pastures and fences. The old highway was not reclaimed, and all the way north is the Backbone of the World to the west.

Arriving at the intersection of U.S. 89 and U.S. Highway 2, means there are four miles to Browning.

The massacre site is about 70 miles to the east, south of Dunkirk. A 15-minute web video shows what the conditions were like in January 2016 when some tribal members traveled there on horseback. "The Bear River Massacre (Blackfeet)" by Rez Reel, (created by Ron Ingraham) on YouTube dated Feb. 3, 2017, is an effective introduction for the non-Indian.

Turning east and four miles to Browning, one sees signs of commerce, a horse herd, billboards, a railroad, a roadside exhibit sign, the road to Heart Butte and the town with BCC on the right.

Croff is a fifth generation descendant of Heavy Runner through his son Dick Kipp. Joe Kipp, the scout who accompanied Col. Eugene Baker's contingent to the river bluffs overlooking Heavy Runner's campsite, was so remorseful, Croff said, that he adopted Dick and two of his siblings.

Horace Clarke, Malcolm's son, accompanied Baker to avenge his father's murder, but several years later he advocated for compensation for the band's confiscated horses. Choteau's co-founder Alfred Hamilton advocated, too. He had married a Blackfeet woman, and his daughter lived on the reservation and was married to Horace's son.

Dick Kipp died in 1935 never having his claim for compensation, sent to the government in 1914, granted.

"They are our ancestors. It is incumbent on us to not let history die," Croff said, explaining that non-Indians have said to "get over it," but to that she said, the late First Nations elder, Narcisse Blood, replied, "Don't you think I would, if I could?"

But Croff added that the focus would be on healing, to face what happened and to embrace the strength and temerity of the people who crawled away from the place of death to walk frostbitten to Fort Benton.

Johnson gave an inspirational talk to the mostly college-age students in the audience. "Your ancestors did not survive so that you could drop out of school," he said, before explaining the teaching tools for restorative practices that are being used on the reservation. These include oral history, unconditional positive regard for each other, the practice of listening as well as talking, extended families, ceremonies and language. "Put culture in lessons every day," Johnson said.

Surname Index